Where Does Christian Freedom End?

Where Does Christian Freedom End?

An Exegetical Commentary on First Corinthians Eight

By

Spiros Zodhiates, Th.D.

AMG
PUBLISHERS
Chattanooga, TN 37422

Where Does Christian Freedom End?

An Exegetical Commentary on First Corinthians Eight

ISBN 0-89957-469-6

Printed in the United States of America

03 02 01 00 99 98 –A– 7 6 5 4 3 2

To my beloved nephew, Dr. Demosthenes Katsarkas, director of St. Luke's Hospital, Thessaloniki, Greece, whose talents and dedication to excellence are notable in the development of that institution, and whose Christian character is exemplary.

Contents

Preface

Corinth was filled with temples where the people sacrificed animals to idols they considered to be gods. Thus, when Paul preached the gospel in Corinth (Acts 18:1–17) and both Jews and Gentiles were saved, he had also the task of discipling the Christians in matters concerning the idols they had once worshiped.

Now that these converts believed in the true God and forsook idols as Jesus Christ became their Lord and the true God became their Father, Paul taught them that the idols considered as gods by the heathen were nonentities. They were mere figments of the imagination of man.

Paul stresses the reality of the one God versus the unreality of many gods. Jesus Christ through His miraculous conception, life, death, and resurrection revealed the true God.

A practical question faced by the Christian converts of Corinth regarded the food they should eat. The meats sacrificed to idols were available in the marketplace for purchase and consumption by all, including the Christians. Since these meats were cheaper and the idols were considered nonentities by the Christians, Paul believed and taught that eating these meats was up to each individual Christian conscience. There could be no apostolic decree on the subject. Paul claimed that food does not commend us to God, nor does it detract from the relationship of man to God (v. 8). The Christians who considered the idols to which these sacrifices were made as nonentities could feel free to eat them.

There was, however, another related and important consideration in eating meats that had been sacrificed to idols. How was it going to affect the "weak" brother? Was it going to offend him? He may not have full knowledge of the situation that idols are nonentities.

The informed Christian should consider not only his right to eat, but his duty to his weak brother who only knows the fact that these meats were from sacrifices to idols and believes they should be avoided.

In the sinful society in which a Christian lives, he should not prefer that which he has the right to choose, but that which will benefit others in a way pleasing to God. A Christian, therefore, subjugates his right to his duty. The guiding mechanism is a pure and benevolent conscience. What Paul writes in 1 Corinthians 8 helps to develop the conscience to the point that the believer does not merely do that which pleases himself, but that which is beneficial for others and for the glory of God.

SPIROS ZODHIATES

An Overview of First Corinthians

Author: Paul the apostle, author of thirteen other epistles to various individuals and congregations.

Date: About A.D. 55.

Recipients: The congregation Paul had established in Corinth.

Place: From Ephesus.

Theme: Paul had received news about the Corinthian brethren from several sources (1 Cor. 1:11; 7:1; 16:17). The church was afflicted with many of the problems that face young churches and new converts. The apostle, under the inspiration of the Holy Spirit, decided to write this urgent letter to admonish and instruct the church. Among other topics he discussed: the necessity of church discipline (5:1–13); divisions and disputes among Christians (1:10–16; 6:1–11); matters of conscience (8:1–13; 10:19–33); the support of preachers (9:1–27); abuses of the Lord's Supper (10:16–17, 21; 11:17–34); the misuse of spiritual gifts (12:1—14:40); and the importance of the resurrection of Jesus Christ (15:1–58).

An Outline of First Corinthians

In the days of the apostle Paul, Corinth was the capital city of the Roman province of Achaia and the glory of Greece. Though its great ancient splendor had been destroyed by the Romans in 120 B.C., the city was rebuilt under Julius Caesar and restored to wealth and luxury under Augustus. Among all the cities of the world, however, it was most well known for its lewdness. The apostle Paul lived in Corinth for eighteen months (Acts 18:11). After his departure, Paul went to Ephesus. During his three-year stay there, he heard reports of wickedness and division within the Corinthian church. In an effort to correct these evils, Paul wrote several letters to them, including the epistle of First Corinthians.

1:1–9	The introductory remarks of Paul.
1:10–16	Paul condemns the divisions in the church and exhorts its members to unity.
1:17—2:16	Paul defends his ministry. He has preached the wisdom of Christ crucified. This wisdom is foolishness to the world, but is the glory of all those to whom the Spirit of God has revealed the truthfulness of it.
3:1–5	Paul declares that the simplicity of his teaching was due to the carnal state of the Corinthians, which state is clearly evidenced by their divisions.
3:6–23	Jesus Christ is the only foundation. Ministers are mere servants; the work is God's.
4:1–6	The duty of ministers is faithfulness.
4:6–21	Paul contrasts the arrogance and conceit of the false teachers to the humility and sacrifice of the apostles. Using his unique position as their spiritual father, Paul calls on the Corinthian believers to be discerning.
5:1–13	Flagrant, sexual immorality was being practiced by one of the members of the congregation. Paul reproves

	their lack of discipline and calls for expulsion of the guilty party.
6:1–11	Christians should not bring their legal disputes before heathen judges.
6:12–20	Paul reprimands the perversion of the principle of Christian liberty to excuse fornication. Our bodies belong to the Lord and should be devoted to His glory.
7:1–17	Paul answers their questions about marriage.
7:18–24	Paul advises that, provided they are not immoral or unlawful, our social positions should remain intact after coming to Christ.
7:25–40	Paul answers their questions about virgins and widows.
8:1–13	Christian liberty and conscience: was it lawful to eat meat that had been sacrificed to false gods?
9:1–23	Paul declares the right of ministers to be faithfully supported by their congregation.
9:24—10:13	Exhortations to self-denial.
10:14—11:1	While the purchase of meat offered to idols is a matter of conscience, attendance at the heathen feasts of sacrifice is idolatry, even if such was not their intention.
11:2–16	Men and women should take care to conform to the customs of dress in their community that assure modesty and properly reflect the man to be "the glory of God" and the woman to be "the glory of the man."
11:17–34	Paul exhorts the Corinthians to properly partake of the Lord's Supper.
12:1–31	Paul answers their questions about spiritual gifts. He reminds them that they are all members of one body. God has distributed these gifts so that each member may perform the function it is designed for.

13:1–13	Love [*agápe* {26}] is superior to all other gifts.
14:1–25	The gift of prophecy is more valuable than the gift of tongues.
14:26–40	Principles for orderly public worship.
15:1–34	Paul proves the fact of the resurrection of Christ. It is the foundation of our faith and the surety of our own resurrection.
15:35–58	Paul explains the nature of our resurrection.
16:1–9	Paul's specific instructions for the collection of monies from several Greek congregations for the poverty-stricken saints in Palestine.
16:10–12	Recommendations for Timothy and Apollos to be accepted by the Corinthians.
16:13–24	Paul's final admonition to them to stand firm in the faith. Salutation.

1 Cor. 8:1 | From What Perspective Do You Make Judgments?

Concerning the meat sacrificed to idols, we perceive that all have knowledge. Knowledge puffs up, but love edifies.

In this eighth chapter of 1 Corinthians, Paul responds to questions posed to him by the believers in Corinth concerning meats which had been sacrificed to idols. His previous concern was in regard to marriage to which he responded in the seventh chapter of 1 Corinthians.

One of the problems which faced the Corinthian Christians was the question of their attitude toward those Christians who were eating these meats sacrificed to idols. This affected their social life. Much of the meat sold in the market had been offered to idols, and it was commonly served throughout the city.

It might have been supposed that the question was settled by the apostolic decree of the Jerusalem Council which stated, "that you abstain from meats offered to idols, and from blood, and from things strangled, and from fornication. . . ." (Acts 15:29). But, in this total discussion of the problem, no allusion at all is made to any relevant decree.

Paul's Antagonism to Idolatry

Paul's revulsion to idols and idolatry was first expressed when he visited Athens on his way to Corinth: "And while Paul waited for them at Athens, his spirit was stirred in him [*parōxúneto* {3947}, to rouse to anger or indignation], when he saw the city wholly given to idolatry" (Acts 17:16). The word in Greek is *kateídōlon* (2712), full of idols, and it comes from the intensive *katá* (2596), full of, and *eídōlon* (1497), idol. An idol is a representation, an image of something corporeal or imaginary. This can be a statue of a real or an imaginary personality or an idea. These images of real personalities or imaginary ideas were set up for worship as gods.

For instance, when Moses delayed his descent from Mount Sinai, the Israelites made a calf as a representative deity and offered sacrifices to it and rejoiced in the works of their own hands (Ex. 32; Acts 7:41). Thus a calf made with human hands became an idol to whom sacrifices were offered.

In 1 Corinthians 12:2 Paul calls such idols made with hands "dumb idols." The word used for "dumb" is *áphōna* (880), voiceless, from the privative alpha, *a*–(1), without, and *phōnḗ* (5456), voice.

In Revelation 9:20 John calls them "the works of their [human] hands, that they should not worship devils [*daimónia* {1140}, little demons, used in the New Testament regarding the heathen gods as in Acts 17:18]; and idols of gold, and silver, and brass, and stone, and of wood; which neither can see, nor hear, nor walk."

Worship of Dumb Idols Is Abhorrent

Paul calls the worship of such idols a sacrilege. It is bad enough to make idols out of material things with one's own hands, but what an offense against the true God to bow down before them and worship them as gods! "You that abhor idols, do you commit sacrilege?" The word for "sacrilege" is *hierosuleís* (2416), found only in Romans 2:22, and derived from *hierós* (2413), sacred, meaning only for the true God, and *suláō* (4813), to spoil, rob, plunder. The verb *hierosuléō* means to take the sacred worship that belongs only to God and give it to idols which are false gods.

In Corinth there were temples dedicated especially to idols called *eidṓleia* (1493), idol temples (1 Cor. 8:10), where animal sacrifices were offered to the idols. How indignant Paul must have been to find the Corinthians not only worshiping these idols, but sacrificing animals to them as part of their worship.

The heathen people of Corinth, after offering an animal for sacrifice, gave a portion to the priests. The remaining part was either displayed by the owner for sale in the market, usually cheaper than other meat, or became the occasion of a banquet, either in the temple or at the owner's house.

The Use of Meats Sacrificed to Idols

The question which believers were asking Paul was not concerned with the sacrifices made to idols in the temples, but whether they were permitted to eat the meat left over from such sacrifices. Could they eat it with a clear conscience?

This concerned Gentile believers. While they did not need to become Jewish by keeping the ceremonial law, it was agreed upon by the apostles in Acts 15:20 that they give them written instructions to "abstain [*apéchesthai*, the present infinitive of *apéchō* {568}, abstain, keep away from] from pollutions of idols [*alisgēmátōn*, the plural genitive of *alísgēma* {234}, pollution by unclean or forbidden food]." What made such meat unclean was that it was offered as a sacrifice to idols, not that it was spoiled in itself and could harm them. The pollution was by association.

There were some Corinthian Christians, however, who would argue that since the meat was good, eating it could not harm them; so why should they not eat it, especially since it was cheaper than other meat?

Understanding the Facts

Here is Paul's answer: "We perceive that all have knowledge." The verb in Greek is *oídamen*, the present perfect of *eídō* (1492), to perceive, know intuitively, used as a present tense. It means that we do not just simply know and are aware of the facts, but that we judge the whole situation as believers in Jesus Christ. We have the capacity of rendering the proper evaluation of the situation. The noun is *gnṓsin*, the accusative of *gnṓsis* (1108), knowledge of the facts. We all (*pántes*, the plural of *pás* [3956], each one as an individual concerned about this matter) have the facts of this situation.

What is important in this matter, Paul seems to be implying, is how we apply these facts from our point of view. "All things are permissible to me, but all are not expedient" (1 Cor. 6:12; 10:23).

There are three questions to consider when evaluating facts or practices:

I. Will that which I do or eat become something that will master me? This is stated in 1 Corinthians 6:12: "All things are permissible for me, but I will not be brought under the power of any."

II. Is it going to build me up, realizing that there is only one foundation, Jesus Christ (1 Cor. 3:10–17; 10:23)?

III. How will it affect other Christians (Rom. 14:1–13)? I cannot disregard the fact that my life is on "candid camera." Will what I do build up the lives of other Christians, especially those with a weak faith?

And then Paul gives a general statement which ought to guide us in the judgments that we make. In every situation, first come the facts of the case. This is the *gnṓsis*, the knowledge of the facts. But he asserts that knowing facts alone can puff one up. The verb translated "puffs up" is used exclusively by the apostle Paul (1 Cor. 4:6, 18, 19; 5:2; 8:1; 13:4; Col. 2:18). It is the word *phusióō* (5448) from *phusáō*, to breathe, blow, inflate, puff up. In the New Testament it is used figuratively, speaking of pride or self-conceit. It derives from *phúsis* (5449), nature. The natural tendency of man is that the more he knows, the more puffed up he becomes.

In his great hymn of love (1 Cor. 13:4), the apostle writes, "Love vaunteth not itself, does not puff itself up." The two verbs used here are *perpereúetai* (used only in this verse), the present indicative middle/passive of *perpereúomai* (4068) from *pérperos*, a braggart, one who boasts over what he has or knows; and *phusioútai*, the present indicative middle of *phusióō*, to puff up. The negative "not" is *ou* (3756) which is an absolute negative. The love which God plants in a believer's heart absolutely does not boast and does not puff itself up. Paul is telling us in 1 Corinthians 8:1 that in sinful man, knowledge can become pride.

The duty of the believer is to approach the matter from the standpoint of others when deciding whether to eat meats sacrificed to idols. Self should take second place. This can be applied to anything which the believer is free to partake of or do. The pleasure it will bring to the individual or how it will inflate his image is not to be considered, rather the good it will bring to others is to be of paramount importance. Whether it is drink or food or feast day or whatever, the consideration of others should predominate.

<u>LESSONS</u>:

1. The Corinthian Christians sought apostolic advice concerning the custom of eating meats sacrificed to idols.
2. They did not take it for granted that an accepted custom was right to continue as consistent with Christian principles.

3. Knowing the facts about sacrifices made to idols was not sufficient in itself.
4. Knowledge of facts makes one proud, because one may think he knows more than another.
5. There is a further dimension to behavior, and it is that of love. One who is a Christian ought not to ask how much his knowledge will excuse that which benefits self, but how his actions will affect those who look at him as an example.

1 Cor. 8:2 | *He Who Thinks He Knows It All Has a Lot to Learn*

But suppose someone thinks he has perceived anything, in no way has he known anything even as he ought to know;

The conjunction of contrast is *dé* (1161), but, and is used in this verse with *ei* (1487), if, which expresses a supposition separate from all experience and indicates a mere subjective possibility: but suppose someone thinks he has perceived (TR, MT) something. The "someone" (*tis* [5100], an enclitic indefinite pronoun meaning "anyone") indicates an undefined person. The verb "thinks" is *dokeí*, the third person singular present indicative of *dokéō* (1380), to think or imagine, expressing the subjective mental estimate or opinion of a person about a certain matter. The infinitive is *eidénai* (TR, MT), the perfect active infinitive of *oída* (1492), to perceive. To perceive means to have gathered the facts that are available to arrive at a conclusion, obviously an erroneous one in this instance. The intimation is that this "someone" is settled in his opinion, and that although it is just an opinion, yet there is an objective finality to it—a "don't trouble me with the facts; my mind is already made up" attitude.

We Cannot Know Anything in Its Totality

Such a person is not to be trusted because there may be certain facts of which he is not aware. The conclusion about such a person is that he never has known all there is to know about a thing.

The Greek word for "not" in the TR and MT is *oudépō* (3764), never yet, and it is made up of the absolute negative *ou* (3756), not; the adversative *dé*, but, and; and *pō* (4452), yet, even. *Oudépō* therefore means "absolutely not yet." This word, used only in composition as in the Nestle's Text, is replaced in Nestle's by *oúpō* (3768) meaning not yet or at any particular time. To strengthen the absoluteness of the case, Paul adds *oudén*, not anything, the neuter of *oudeís* (3762), not a one, meaning "nothing."

The verb is *égnōke*, the perfect active indicative of *ginṓskō* (1097), to experientially know. The verb *ginṓskō* can mean to know in a beginning sense, to start the process of learning, or, in a completed sense, to finish learning something. This verb is to be taken in a completed sense. Such a person has not completely learned something. Therefore, there must be an "if" about the finality of our conclusions, for there may be facts yet to be discovered. Let us not forget the words of wisdom found in 1 Corinthians 13:9: "For we know [*ginṓskomen*, experientially know] in part." At no time may we ever claim that we know all there is to be known about a particular thing. This is why we need revelation since full discovery is absolutely impossible. Thus John says, "And you have anointment from the Holy [One], and you perceive [*oídate*, perceive; not the word *ginṓskete*, experientially know] all things" (1 John 2:20). We have a way of arriving at the absolute truth, but this is only by revelation (John 14:6; 1 John 5:20) and not by the discovery of knowledge, because at best we only know partially.

The perfect tense of the verb *égnōke* is significant. It should be translated "has known" or "has learned." In our earthly sojourn we can never say at any given time that we have all the experiential knowledge. That is impossible because, as John says in 1 John 3:2, "Beloved, we are now children of God, and it was not yet [*oúpō*] revealed *nor was it yet made apparent* [*ephanerṓthē*, the aorist passive of *phaneróō* {5319}, to manifest, make apparent] what we shall be."

"Even as [*kathṓs* {2531}, just as, derived from *katá* {2596}, according as; and *hōs* {5613}, in the same manner, likewise] he ought [*deí* {1163}, must, is a necessity or inevitable in the nature of things] to know [*gnṓnai*, the aorist active infinitive of *ginṓskō*, to experientially know]." At no time can anyone conclude that he has acquired all the knowledge that is to be had and thus arrive at an irrefutable conclusion (*eidénai*). What the apostle says in this verse constitutes the basis of science and education. A scientist is one who arrives at Socrates' dictum: "I get old ever learning." Furthermore, there is never a point in time when one can arrogantly boast, I have learned all there is to learn, therefore I have learned in full. Experiential knowledge about anything is always lacking. The finality of knowledge comes as a result of one's relationship with God as His child (1 John 2:20; 3:2).

The Principle of Love

Whether we as believers should or should not eat of the meats sacrificed to idols is not a matter of divine revelation, but is a matter of human conclusion according to the knowledge we have on the matter. The Lord has not said eat or don't eat. Let the principle be one of love and not of knowledge.

<u>LESSONS</u>:

1. We must recognize that our human conclusions are incomplete, for they are based on partial knowledge of facts.

2. Only through divine revelation can we have absolute truth about anything.
3. We know only in part, because we are creatures of time and space.
4. God is eternal and omniscient and is therefore the only One qualified to know the true nature of the things and people He created. This knowledge of His can only be communicated to us humans through faith in Him. We cannot know the absolute, but we can believe it as long as the Revealer is trustworthy. Jesus Christ is such a Revealer of truth because of His proven resurrection (1 John 5:20).
5. When we believe in Him, we receive His love and become communicators of it (1 John 5:1).
6. We love God not because we know Him fully, but because through believing in Jesus Christ, we respond to His love. Belief is a response to His love.

1 Cor. 8:3 — *The Lord Recognizes Our Love*

But if one loves God, the same is known by Him.

The supposition of one's love for God is subjective. "If" is *ei* (1487), the conjunction of subjective reality: "**If** one loves God." Love, indeed, is subjective. It is known only by its fruits (1 Cor. 13:4–8) which may be observed by others.

God Knows the Measure of Our Love

God, however, who created love as an accompaniment of faith, does not have to wait for the works of faith and love to prove its existence, for He who knows the heart knows all things. The believing one (*ho pisteúōn*) is the loving one (*ho agapṓn*) (see 1 John 5:1). The moment a person believes, he begins to love.

The word for "love" is *agapá*, the present subjunctive of *agapáō* (25), to love. The present subjunctive indicates the permanence of love. Although it is permanent, it is not static, but progressive. Our verse does not say **loved** (*ēgápēse*) but **loves** God. This love is continuous as is faith. We come again to 1 John 5:1, the believing one (*ho pisteúōn*, the present participle of *pisteúō* [4100], to believe), and the loving one (*ho agapṓn*, the present participle of *agapáō,* to love). In the phrase, "if one loves **the** God," the definite article before the word "God" (*Theós*

[2316]) indicates God the Father (John 1:1b) as distinct from Christ (John 20:28; Heb. 1:8). Before one has the opportunity to show the love of God in a demonstrable manner, he has been accepted (*égnōstai*, the third person singular perfect passive indicative of *ginṓskō* [1097], to experientially know) by God, which is equivalent to being known.

The verb *égnōstai* here means to have been accepted by the Father, or acknowledged by God. This refers to the acceptance by God of our love which is subsequent to the exercise of our faith. This acceptance comes before we have the opportunity to manifest our effective faith in love.

While God does not have to wait for the demonstration of our love to find out whether or not it is genuine, our fellow Christians can tell only by observing our actions whether our lives are directed by His love or not. Our consideration of others in matters such as eating meats sacrificed to idols is one way they can know. When His love is shown in our daily lives, He recognizes it because it is the love that He has imparted to us.

His love becomes part of our nature. We do not demonstrate mere acts of love, but a loving lifestyle to our fellow human beings, and especially our brethren in Christ (1 John 4:20, 21).

LESSONS:

1. We cannot say that we love God and ignore the effects our lives have on our fellow human beings and especially on Christian brethren.
2. Our love for God is not a natural love, but emanates from His love implanted in us through faith in Jesus Christ.
3. Belief in our hearts is acknowledged by God, and we express it not merely in acts of love, but in a transformed nature (2 Pet. 1:4).

1 Cor. 8:4 | *Idols Are Not God*

Concerning, therefore, the eating of meats sacrificed to idols, we perceive that absolutely no idol in the world ***represents a real existence*** *and that* ***there is no*** *God* ***that*** *is different than the one* ***true*** *God.*

"Concerning [*perí* {4012}, exactly the same word we have in v. 1], therefore, the eating. . . ." In other words, how do the general statements which Paul enunciated previously apply to this particular discussion on eating meats sacrificed to idols?

The True God Is Spirit

The first thing to consider is whether the idols to whom these sacrifices were made are real beings. They are not, Paul asserts. They would not and could not be "God" because "God is spirit" (John 4:24). And in the words of John 1:1, "In the beginning was the Word [*Lógos* {3056}, logic, intelligence]." This immaterial self–existent God became flesh (John 1:14) and received material form.

Jesus Christ was that immaterial personality who took upon Himself a tangible form. He is never called an idol, nor is He the idol (*eídōlon* [1497]) of God. The word "idol" is used for a statue of a man or even a concept of the mind, an imaginary deity in some material shape. But if God is the product of man's imagination, then he must be a creation of man and not man's Creator. Thus Paul states that an idol is nothing real in the world, and it represents something that is not the true God.

Jesus Christ Is the Image of God—Idols Are Representatives of What Is Thought of as God

In Romans 1 verse 23 we are told about a characteristic of the true God: "And [fallen men] changed the glory of the incorruptible God into an image made like to corruptible man, and to birds, and four–footed beasts, and creeping things." The true God is called "incorruptible" (*áphthartos* [862]) and man is called "corruptible" (*phthartós* [5349]). *Phthorá* (5356) is corruption or decay, and it refers to something material, for instance, the body of man (1 Cor. 15:42, 50). A near synonym of *phthorá* is *diaphthorá* (1312), also meaning utter decay or corruption throughout. The body of Jesus, unlike our human body, did not experience corruption (*diaphthorá*) at His death (Acts 2:27, 31). Hebrews 2:14, when correctly translated, makes this quite clear: "Inasmuch, therefore, as the children have shared in the flesh and blood, even He [Jesus] very closely [*paraplēsíōs* {3898}] partook of the same [flesh and blood]; so that through death He might destroy the one having dominion of death, that is, the devil." This means that Jesus' body with flesh and blood was capable of dying (Phil. 2:8), yet did not decompose at death as ours does. He was the incorruptible God who came into the world in the likeness (*homoiṓmati*, the dative of *homoíōma* [3667], resemblance, likeness) of the image (*eikónos* [1504], picture) of corruptible man.

We could say that the *homeíōma*, the resemblance, is a portrait while the *eikṓn* is the visible photograph of the One who is essentially spirit, intelligence (*Lógos*). It is the actual image of the real expression. The invisible God became visible. Second Corinthians 4:4 tells us that Jesus Christ is the image (*eikṓn*) of God, not the *homoíōma*, the likeness of God. *Eídōla* (idols) are representations of something that actually does not exist in the world. They are copies of what men imagine to be deity, whether they are representations or images of corruptible man or birds or four–footed beasts and creeping things. They are material, hence corruptible, because they are made of wood or silver, gold or brass, or any other substance.

In His second commandment God said, "You shall not make unto yourself any graven image [*pes̱el* {6459, OT}, carved idol or graven image], or any likeness [t^{e}*mūnah* {8544, OT}, likeness, similitude] of anything that is in heaven above, or that is in the earth beneath, or that is in the water under the earth" (Ex. 20:4). The manufacture of such idols is forbidden since they are merely figments of the imagination. "You shalt not bow down yourself to them, nor serve them" (Ex. 20:5). Deuteronomy 4:15–19 is even more explicit by saying:

> Take you, therefore, good heed unto yourselves . . . lest you corrupt yourselves, and make you a graven image, the similitude of any figure, the likeness of male or female, the likeness of any beast that is on the earth, the likeness of any winged fowl that flies in the air, the likeness of anything that creeps on the ground, the likeness of any fish that is in the waters beneath the earth. And lest you lift up your eyes unto heaven, and when you see the sun, and the moon, and the stars, even all the host of heaven, should be driven to worship them, and serve them, which the Lord your God has divided unto all nations under the whole heaven.

The second characteristic of idols is not only that they are corruptible, they are also dumb. "You know that you were Gentiles, carried away unto these dumb idols even as you were led" (1 Cor. 12:2). The Greek word translated "dumb" is *áphōna* (880) derived from the privative alpha, *a–* (1), without, and *phōnḗ* (5456), voice, thus meaning voiceless, not having the power of speech. Idols can neither hear nor respond to the worshipers' cries. These are different than the living God. He is called "the living Father" (John 6:57), meaning the One who has life in Himself. "For it is written, 'As I live,' says the Lord, 'every knee shall bow to me, and every tongue shall confess to God.' So then every one of us shall give an account of himself to God" (Rom. 14:11, 12; Sept.: Num. 14:21, 28). God is alive as opposed to idols which are nonexistent (1 Cor. 12:2). "And what agreement has the temple of God with idols? For you are the temple **of the living God**; as God has said, 'I will dwell in them, and walk in them; and I will be their God, and they shall be my people' " (2 Cor. 6:16). Paul, in writing to the Thessalonian believers, says, "For they themselves show of us what manner of entering in we had unto you, and how you turned to God from idols to serve **the living and true God**" (1 Thess. 1:9; Sept.: Deut. 5:26; 2 Kgs. 19:16).

Thus when Paul writes that absolutely no idol **exists** in the world, nor **represents a real existence,** he means idols are merely a material representation of something imaginary that has no life in itself. Idols are dead, nonexistent, while the true God is spirit, not corruptible matter, who is alive and gives life (John 1:4; 14:6; 1 John 1:2; 5:20).

No Other Different God Exists

Another thing that the apostle Paul wants us to realize through this discussion concerning meats sacrificed to idols is that no other different God exists. The word for "other different" is *héteros* (2087), which means another who is different. Since the idols in the world are simply material and dead, they are not the real God. The verb *eí* (the present indicative of *eimí* [1510], to be) is implied. The verb "is" is also implied in the previous statement "that no idol [is] in the world," meaning something representing the true God. These idols represent an imaginary god other than the true One, "for there [is] no other **different** God." In the Greek idiom, when the verb is missing, then the truth expressed transcends particular situations and expresses eternal truth. An example of that is Hebrews 13:8, "Jesus Christ *is* the same yesterday, and today, and forever." The verb "is" is implied to show that the character of God is always the same, but not necessarily His actions. These vary according to what He wants to accomplish and for whom.

"There [is] no god *that is* different than the one *true* God." The Greek expression is *ei mḗ heís* (*ei* [1487], the suppositional conjunction of mere subjective possibility; *mḗ* [3361], the relative subjective negative "not"; *heís* [1520], one in number). This is a confirmation of monotheism as opposed to the polytheism of idolatry. If idols are gods, there are many gods, but Jehovah is One: "Hear, O Israel! The Lord our God is one Lord" (Deut. 6:4). There is no other like Him. All the idols that have ever been created by man are not gods. If they were, there would be more than one God which is perceptually impossible (*oídamen*, we perceive, which is the verb used in this verse). Paul is not dealing here with the revelation of the Lord Jesus that the One God is in three persons, each One being God (Matt. 28:19). There are not three Gods, but only One in three Persons.

LESSONS:

1. In our consideration as to whether we as Christians ought to eat of meats sacrificed to idols, we must first examine what an idol is.
2. We must conclude that idols are not real beings. Idols do indeed exist, but that which they represent is nonexistent.
3. Idols, being unreal, cannot answer any of our questions regarding this life or the next, while the real God has spoken through His Son, the Lord Jesus Christ (John 3:34; 6:63; 7:17, 18; 8:28, 40, 49, 50; 14:10;

16:13). His eternal name is *Lógos*, intelligence, immaterial personality, Spirit, which also means Word, expression.

4. If idols are nothing, then meats sacrificed to idols are nothing.
5. If idols are considered to be gods, then they are different than the real God, for God is One.
6. Jesus Christ revealed God to be three Persons in One—God the Father, God the Son, and God the Holy Spirit (Matt. 28:19).
7. The real God lives, speaks, and imparts His grace to those who believe in Him. He makes them partakers of His nature (2 Pet. 1:4) and thus possessors and demonstrators of His love (1 John 5:1).

1 Cor. 8:5 | *Though Many Are Called Gods, There Is Only One*

And, therefore, even if indeed there are many ***called*** *gods, either in heaven or on earth (then we should indeed* ***conclude*** *there are many gods and many lords);*

This verse confirms that idolaters believe in polytheism, that there are many "gods" and many "lords." This is the inevitable conclusion that we would arrive at if we accept the notion that idols are gods, and it would be a denial that there is only one true God and Lord of all. One cannot be both a polytheist and a monotheist.

"And therefore, even if indeed [*kaí* {2532}, and, even; *gár* {1063}, therefore; *eíper* {1512}, if indeed, derived from the suppositional conjunction of subjective possibility outside of experience, which is from *ei* {1487}, if, and *per* {4007}, perhaps, assuming the supposition as real which becomes 'indeed'] there are many called gods." Paul does not say that there are many gods, but "there are many **called** [*legómenoi*, the present passive participle of *légō* {3004}, to say] gods" by those who make them and worship them.

Suppose Idols Are Gods

The subjective conclusion then would be that there are many gods. It would make no difference whether they are in heaven or on the earth. (However, we know that they are imaginary gods, existing only in the minds of those who think of them as such.) The conclusion of this supposition is likewise subjective: "then we should indeed [*hṓsper* {5618}, as indeed, therefore indeed], *conclude* there are [*eisí*, are, the third person plural present indicative of *eimí* {1510}, to be] many [*polloí*, the plural of *polús* {4183}, much] gods [*theoí*, the plural of *theós* {2316}, god] and many lords [*kúrioi*, the plural of *kúrios* {2962}, lord]."

If we attribute deity to idols, then the result is that there are innumerable so-called gods and lords. This is polytheism, while the main doctrine of Judaism and Christianity is that there is one God and Lord who is also the Father of Jesus Christ (Eph. 1:2). Jesus Christ who has always been with the Father, being the unique One, "exegeted" Him (John 1:18; see the author's exegetical study on John 1:1–18 entitled *Was Christ God?*). If there are many lords, there cannot be oneness of purpose. The uniqueness of God precludes the multiplicity of gods for God alone must be Lord.

LESSONS:

1. Accepting the supposition that idols are gods, then the fact that there are innumerable different idols would suggest that there must be innumerable gods. We know this supposition is false!
2. If each idol represents a different god, there cannot be oneness of purpose.
3. If there are many lords, which is a sheer impossibility (Deut. 6:4), man's heart would become a battleground of divided loyalties.

1 Cor. 8:6 — *One God—One Lord Jesus Christ*

Yet for us ***there exists*** *one God* ***who is*** *the Father, of whom all things* ***proceed*** *and we* ***exist*** *for Him, and one* ***who is the*** *Lord Jesus Christ, through whom all things* ***exist****, and we through Him.*

Here we have a statement which all Christians believe, but which was particularly relevant to Paul and the believers of Corinth, for it stood in contrast to the belief of idolaters. The resultant conclusion of attributing deity to an idol, since there are many idols, is that there are many gods. Any conclusion based on a wrong assumption must also be wrong.

The Christian Belief in God

"Yet for us [*allá* {235}, but, contrariwise, howbeit, nevertheless; *hēmín*, the dative plural first person pronoun of *egṓ* {1473}, I, meaning 'to us' or 'for us' believers who are not idolaters] *there exists* one God." Verse 4 tells us that there are absolutely no idols in the world which represent objective reality. If the idol represents an imaginary god, it must be a different god than the real God in whom Christians believe.

In 1 John 5:20, 21, John uses the word *alēthinṓ*, the dative of *alēthinós* (228), true, as opposed to *pseudḗs* (5571), false, to warn us to guard ourselves from idols: "And we know [*oídamen*, the present perfect of *eídō* {1492}, to perceive, used with present meaning] that the Son of God is come, and has given us an understanding, that we may know Him that is **true**, and we are in Him that is **true**, even in His Son Jesus Christ. This is the **true** God, and eternal life. Little children, keep yourselves from idols. Amen" (1 John 5:20, 21. See author's exposition of these verses in *The Epistles of John*.) John is stressing that we can only know experientially (*ginṓskō*) the true God through the revelation of a real witness, and that witness was Jesus Christ who took our human form and spoke in our language so that we could understand (*diánoian* [1271], intelligence) Him. Our faith, therefore, is based on the true witness of an acceptable Person who claimed to be the Way for us to know the otherwise unknowable; the Truth which we could not otherwise discover, and the Life which we could acquire in no other way but through Him. This only one true God said in John 14:6, "I am the way, the truth and the life."

God Is an Objective Reality

"*There exists* one God." "There exists" is not in the Greek text, but is implied. The Greek says, "But for us one God, the Father." The verb is implied. Previously, in verse 4, Paul spoke of the non-existence of what the idol represents, for it is merely the figment of man's imagination and is thus lacking objective reality. But this objective reality of the God of the Bible exists. As John says in 1 John 1:1, "That which was from the beginning, which we have heard, which we have seen with our eyes, which we have looked upon, and our hands have handled, of the Word of life." This is Jesus Christ who in John 1:1 is called "the Word" (*Lógos* [3056]), and in John 14:6 "the life" (*zōḗ* [2222], inherent life). The disciples involved their senses of hearing, sight, touch, and comprehension, and came to understand, to arrive at the true conclusion.

Jesus was not an idol. An idol cannot speak so that it can be heard (1 Cor. 12:2). Jesus Christ spoke and we could understand Him. Our eyes could see Him. We admired Him (*etheasámetha*, the aorist middle deponent indicative of *theáomai* [2300], to view attentively, admiringly). We touched Him, handled Him. He was alive. He communicated His life to us. "For the life was manifested, and we have seen it, and bear witness, and show unto you that eternal life, which was with the Father, and was manifested unto us" (1 John 1:2). Observe the reference to God as the Father. The revelation of Jesus Christ was to acquaint us with the Father and to enable us to have fellowship (*koinōnía* [2842], participation) with God the Father and His Son, Christ the Lord. (See the chapter on 1 John 1:2 in *The Epistles of John*.)

Only Jesus Christ spoke the words recorded in John 14:9, "He that has seen me has seen the Father." Again, notice that the object of Christ's revelation was to tell us about God the Father.

In John 1:18 we are told that Jesus Christ was described as the unique (*monogenḗs* [3439], the only one of His kind) Son (*huiós* [5207] in the TR and MT) being (*ho ṓn*, the One being, the present participle of *eimí* [1510], to be) in the bosom of the Father. He Himself brought Him out of His concealment (*exēgḗsato*, the third person aorist middle deponent indicative of *exēgéomai* [1834], to lead out). Jesus Christ in His eternal existence as God (John 1:1c) was the only One who was from the beginning who could reveal God to us (Rom. 16:25).

In the phrase "Yet for us there exists one God," note that the word "God" (*Theós* [2316]) does not have the definite article in front of it. "But for us *there exists* one [*heís* {1520}, the masculine numeral one] God." As I have noted in *The Complete Word Study Dictionary: New Testament*, the word "God" without the definite article refers to deity. If it were used with the definite article "the," it would have referred to God the Father (cf. John 1:1b).

In this instance of 1 Corinthians 8:6, "God," not having the definite article, refers to deity which is indeed One—a Triunity, God the Father, God the Son, and God the Holy Spirit. In John 20:28 when Thomas said of Jesus "My Lord and my God," he was recognizing that Jesus was both ruler (*Kúrios* [2962], Lord, Master) and God (*Theós* [2316], deity; cf. Rom. 9:5; Titus 2:13; Heb. 1:8; 1 Pet. 1:2). They are all deity, not differing one from the other in their essence, eternal, self-existent, equal in power, substance, glory, and character. This is explicitly revealed by Jesus Christ, who in His final command in one of His post-resurrection appearances, said, "Having gone, make disciples of all nations, baptizing them in the name [note He did not say 'names'] of the Father and of the Son and of the Holy Spirit" (Matt. 28:19).

The Plural Name of God

In the Hebrew, the equivalent of "God" is *'^{e}lōhīm* (*'El'ōhim̈*) (430, OT) which is plural. Yet it is consistently translated in the Septuagint as *Theós*, "God" in the singular and not in the plural as it is in Hebrew. The Greek verbs which indicate God's activity are always in the singular. The reason for this was that at the time the Septuagint translation was made from the Hebrew to the Greek language (about 200 B.C.), Greek idolatry was the prevailing superstition, especially in Egypt under the Ptolemies. Their gods were regarded as demons or intelligent beings totally separate and distinct from each other. If the translators rendered the name of the true God by the plural *theoí*, gods, they would have given the heathen under Greek culture an idea of God inconsistent with the unity of the divine essence and conformable to their own polytheistic notions. However, by translating the Hebrew *ᵉlōhīm* as "God" followed by singular verbs, they emphasized the unity of God and at the same time did not deny a plurality of persons in the divine nature.

The Trinity in the New Testament

In the New Testament and the Septuagint, *Theós*, God, generally answers to the Old Testament plural name *ᵉlōhīm* and so denotes God the Trinity. See Matthew 4:7: "Thou shall not tempt the Lord, thy God" (cf. Deut. 6:16 in the Hebrew and Sept.), also verse 10 (cf. Deut. 6:3); 22:32 (cf. Ex. 3:6), 37 (cf. Deut. 6:5); Mark 1:14, 15 (cf. Dan. 2:44); 12:29 (cf. Deut. 6:4, 5); John 1:12 (cf. Gen. 6:2); Acts 4:24 (cf. Gen. 1:1 in the Hebrew); 10:34 (cf. Deut. 10:17). It is applied personally, but very rarely, to the Father (John 5:18; 13:3; 16:27 [TR, MT], 30; 2 Cor. 13:14; Phil. 2:6); to the Son (Matt. 1:23; John 1:1; 20:28; Rom. 9:5; 1 Tim. 3:16 [TR]; Titus 2:13; 2 Pet. 1:1; 1 John 5:20); and to the Holy Spirit (Acts 5:3, 4 [cf. Acts 4:24, 25 with Acts 1:16]; 1 Cor. 3:16, 17; 6:19; 2 Cor. 6:16; 2 Pet. 1:21).

While the term "one" God in 1 Corinthians 8:6 is *heís*, the numeral one, in John 10:30 where Jesus said, "I and My Father are one," the Greek word is *hén*, the accusative singular neuter of *heís*—it does not mean that they are the same personality, but they are of the same **essence**, therefore equal. The Lord Jesus claimed equality but not identity with the Father (Matt. 1:23; John 1:1; 20:28; Rom. 9:5; 1 Tim. 3:16 [TR]; Titus 2:13; 2 Pet. 1:1; 1 John 5:20).

God the Father Is the Creator and Sustainer of All Things

The one "God" is first listed as *ho Patḗr*, the Father. "One God of [*ex* or *ek* {1537}, of, indicating the point of origin or source] whom [*hoú*, the genitive singular relative pronoun of *hós* {3739}, which, indicating the oneness of God, that is, the Father who is

God] all things [*tá pánta: tá*, the nominative plural neuter of the article *ho* {3588}, the; *pánta*, the accusative plural neuter adjective of *pás* {3956}, all, meaning each individual thing and all of them in the group of created things, not each evolving from the other but each in its kind {see Gen. 1:11, 12, 21, 24, 25; 6:20; 7:14}] *proceed*." Actually, there is no verb in the Greek referring back to "all things." I have elected to employ the word "proceed": "of whom all things proceed." The KJV assumes the verb to be "are": "Of whom *are* all things." Each thing was created by God the Father for a particular purpose which has been designed by Him. God the Father is not only presented as the preexistent creator of all things, but also the sustainer of all things (Col. 1:17). He made all things like a puzzle, each fitting into its own particular place so that the totality of His creation may function as a whole to accomplish its intended purpose. His fatherhood is eternally conjoined with His divinity, and His divinity is infinitely and eternally conjoined with His fatherhood.

"And we" (*kaí* [2532], and; *hēmeís* [2249], the nominative plural first person of the personal pronoun *egṓ*, I) refers to believers including the apostle Paul. It constitutes the totality of the created and the redeemed people. The totality of the created world is divided into two groups: the fallen creation and the redeemed creation. The redeemed believe that all things exist because they were created and are sustained by God the Father. We who have accepted the redemption designed by deity recognize that the purposes for which God created and sustains us are our redemption and His glory.

The Trinity in Redemption

The Trinity is revealed to us as actively participating in the work of our salvation: "For God [*ho Theós*, God the Father] so loved the world that he gave his unique [*monogenḗs*] Son that whosoever believes in him should not perish, but have everlasting life" (John 3:16). Until Christ was glorified and ascended, the outpouring of the Holy Spirit could not take place. Then as Christ was departing from the world, He revealed a doctrine which clearly associated the Holy Spirit with Himself and the Father in a new and unique way (John 14:16, 17, 25; 15:26; 16:7–15). Acts 5:3, 4, 9 speak of lying against the Holy Spirit as lying against God. The work essential to deity throughout the book of Acts is spoken of as the work of the Holy Spirit (Acts 2:4; 8:29; 10:19; 13:2, 4; 16:6, 7; 20:28). In 1 John 4:13 we read, "By this we experientially know [*ginṓskomen*] that we abide in him and he in us, because of his Spirit which he has given us." Of all God's creation, we human beings who have received the gift of His love (John 1:12) realize the purpose of God's redemptive plan for man. The Father loved us so much that He gave His unique Son to die for our sins, and when we receive Him through God the Holy Spirit, we become children of God. The Father makes the offer, the Son became man to sacrifice Himself, and the Holy Spirit entreats the sinner to believe that by accepting Jesus' sacrifice he is saved.

The Trinity in Creation

When it came to creating man, God did not say, "Let Me make man in My image," but "Let **us** make man in **our** image, after **our** likeness" (Gen. 1:26). While it is one God, when it comes to man's creation, and later to his redemption and indwelling, it is God the Father, God the Son, and God the Holy Spirit who involved themselves. Read 1 Peter 1:2: "Elect according to the foreknowledge of God **the Father**, through sanctification of **the Spirit**, unto obedience and sprinkling of the blood of **Jesus Christ**: Grace unto you, and peace, be multiplied."

Ephesians 2:18 states, "For through him [Christ] we both have access by one Spirit unto the Father." It is because of the work of the Trinity that "Now, therefore, you are no more strangers and foreigners, but fellow citizens with the saints, and of the household of God" (Eph. 2:19).

The Believer Is Indwelt by the Triune God

When we are indwelt by God we are indwelt by the Father (2 Cor. 6:16), by the Son (Rom. 8:10), and by the Holy Spirit (John 14:17; Rom. 8:11).

"And we *exist* for him." The preposition is *eis* (1519), unto, for, and it shows intention, purpose, or aim. The RSV inserts the verb "exist" making the phrase "for whom we exist," and the NIV reads, "we live." It is actually "and we for him." There is an agreement with the phrase with which the verse begins: "And for us" or "unto us one God, the Father, . . . and we for him." We live to fulfill the purpose of our Creator. It is God's purpose and not their own that determines the destiny of men.

Paul is writing to individuals, both Jews and Gentiles, who came into a new relationship with God. This relationship was that of a Father, a concept which was missing for the Jews in the Old Testament and for the Gentiles in their idolatrous background. Observe that the definite article *ho*, the, occurs before the word *Patḗr* (3962), Father. It is God, **the** Father. When we realize what God wants to become in our experience, we are filled with the greatest joy there is available to an individual. In the Old Testament, God is not viewed as being in a father/son relationship with individuals or as the father of mankind in general.

The parable of the Prodigal Son brings to focus the realization of the calamity that results from our detachment from our Father and the joy that comes to His heart and ours on our repentance and return to Him (Luke 15:11–32). "But for us one

God, the Father," from whom through Adam we sought independence and found misery, and to whom we have the privilege of returning in repentance and finding that renewed relationship of Father/son. Now that we have regained the privilege of sonship, we must assume the responsibilities of that relationship: "and we *exist* for him."

The relationship conceived by the Jews was that of a corporate relationship. God was a Father for Israel (Deut. 32:6; Is. 63:16; 64:8; Jer. 3:19, 20; 31:9; Mal. 1:6; 2:10).

In the New Testament, God is referred to as "Father" about 250 times. This is the message the apostle Paul is trying to impress upon the Corinthian Christians—the relationship that exists between each individual believer and God (1 Cor. 4:14–17; 8:6).

The Redeemed Live for God

When Paul, however, says "we *exist* for him," he does not include the Lord Jesus Christ in the "we." In the New Testament we never find the Lord Jesus speaking of God as the common Father of both believers and Himself. He spoke always of "my Father" and "your Father." He never used the phrase "our Father" in a way that linked Himself with the disciples. The relationship of Jesus with God is unique, for He is the eternal Son of God. Yet through Jesus Christ, human beings have been welcomed into a family relationship with God the Father. We are born again into the family of God, whereas Jesus Christ was eternally the Son of the Father (John 1:18). This is why He is called the *monogenḗs*, unique Son, the only one of the kind (John 1:14, 18; 3:16, 18; 1 John 4:9).

At the beginning of each epistle, the Lord Jesus is introduced as the distinct Son (Rom. 1:3; 1 Cor. 1:3; 2 Cor. 1:2; Gal. 1:3; Eph. 1:3; Phil. 1:2; Col. 1:3; 1 Thess. 1:1; 2 Thess. 1:2; 1 Tim.

1:2; 2 Tim. 1:2; Titus 1:4; 1 Pet. 1:3). As believers, we are spoken of as the children of God the Father. Nowhere is Jesus more specific in distinguishing that relationship of God as His Father and ours as His children than when He addressed Mary Magdalene in His post-resurrection appearance to her. He said, ". . . I ascend unto **my** Father, and **your** Father; and to **my** God, and **your** God" (John 20:17). Not that God was different in Himself, but He was different in His relationship to Jesus Christ and to us. He becomes our Father (John 1:12), whereas as far as Jesus Christ in His eternal existence is concerned, He never **became** the son of God as we do. He has always been the Son of God as the present participle *ho ṓn*, "the One being," in John 1:18 declares. (See the book entitled *Was Christ God?*, an exegetical exposition of John 1:1–18 and particularly the section on v. 18.)

We should understand how God acts toward us as our Father. As our Father, He accepts the responsibilities to meet the needs of His family as He sees them: "But my God shall supply all your need according to His riches in glory by Christ Jesus" (Phil. 4:19, cf. Matt. 6:8; Luke 12:30). Notice how, in the next verse, God is referred to as Father. As our Father, we can come to God at any time and for anything (Matt. 6:9; Heb. 4:16).

"And we *exist* for him" (NIV) our verse declares. As we do, we must recognize that He rewards as a father (Matt. 6:1) and also disciplines us (John 15:2; Heb. 12:7–11). At the same time, we recognize that nothing can happen to us without His knowledge and permission or distinctive will (Matt. 10:29, 30). Above everything else, He loves us as the Father (John 16:27).

A Believer Accepts the Lordship of Jesus Christ

Paul then addresses the uniqueness of Jesus Christ and His eternal existence: "And one Lord Jesus Christ." Observe that there is no verb as in the previous statements, "but for us one God, the Father . . . and we for him, and one Lord Jesus Christ." The implied verb can be "is" or "exists." For God to be Father to us as individuals, Jesus Christ has to be Lord. This declares that Christ, as far as we are concerned, appeared in time and space. He had always been self-existent before the creation of the world. The fact that He appeared as the God-Man at Bethlehem when Cyrenius was governor of Syria does not mean that that marked the period of the beginning of His personality as God. While He was on earth, He asserted Himself to be God before even Abraham came to be: "Verily, verily, I say unto you, before Abraham came to be [*genésthai*, the second aorist middle deponent infinitive of *gínomai* {1096}, to begin to be, to come into existence], I am" (John 8:58). (See the use of the verb *gínomai* in John 1:1–18, particularly in vv. 3, 6, 10, 12, 14, and 17 when people or things are spoken of which have a beginning to their existence; also see *Was Christ God?*) In the expression "I am" (*egṓ eimí*), the emphatic "I" (*egṓ*) is used to express exclusive claim to eternity in contrast to any other human being, followed by "am" (the present indicative first person singular of the verb *eimí*, to be).

Unfortunately, the KJV and other translations render both verbs, *gínomai* and *eimí*, as if they were the same word. But they are two different words; *gínomai* meaning to receive existence, to be made, created, and *eimí*, to be. The one is in the aorist, *egéneto*; Abraham and all people and things were created, they received their existence at a certain point in time. The other verb, *eimí*, is in the present tense, meaning I have always been, I have never been made by anybody or anything at any time. This fully agrees with John 1:18 when literally translated: "God no one has ever seen at any time. The only unique Son (TR; MT) who **being** in the bosom of the Father, he himself led him out." Observe that the eternal, unique Son is not indicated as having at a particular time become the Son, but that He ever was (*ho ṓn*: *ho*, the; *ṓn*, the present participle of *eimí*, to be). This refers to His eternal existence, for He never became the Son, He always had been. See John 1:1, 2, 4, 8–10, 15, 18. He became the God-Man for the purpose of identifying Himself with our humanity in order to die for us (Phil. 2:6–8). To prove that He was ever God, the Son, when He became man, uniquely predicted that He was going to die and rise in three days. He was going to raise Himself and show Himself to His disciples (Matt. 16:21; 17:23; 26:32; 28:10, 16; 1 Cor. 15:4–9). The Lord Jesus is said to have been raised by God the Father (Acts 4:10), by Himself (John 2:19; 10:17, 18; Rom. 8:34; 1 Cor. 15:20), and by the Holy Spirit (Rom. 8:11). Thus deity is attributed to the Father, the Son, and the Holy Spirit through the resurrection of the God-Man.

The Uniqueness of Jesus Christ

The apostle Paul asserts the uniqueness of Jesus Christ by saying "and one [*heís*, one, one of a kind] Lord." The word "Lord," used in contradistinction to God the Father, is the Greek *Kúrios* (2962), Lord, Supreme. In the Septuagint, the word *Kúrios* was used to translate the Hebrew word Yahweh (3068, OT), meaning Self-Existent One. It is God's revealed personal name occurring 5,321 times in the Old Testament, and 50 more times in the poetic form *Yāh* (3050, OT). The name is derived from the verb meaning "to be." One cannot but remember how many times the Lord Jesus said, "I am," even as God said unto Moses, "I am that I am" (Ex. 3:13–15). Jehovah God intimates the eternal presence of God. The last words with which the Gospel of Matthew ends are the words of the risen Christ who said, "And behold, **I am** with you all the days unto the consummation of the age. Amen" (28:20).

Note how many times the Lord Jesus in His earthly life affirms and assures His disciples that He is what they need:

I. John 6:35, 48: "I am the bread of life."

II. John 6:41: "I am the bread of life which came down [*ho katabás,* the second aorist participle of *katabaínō* {2597}, to descend, indicating that He was in heaven prior to His incarnation and He voluntarily in His own power came down from heaven at a certain point in time] from heaven."

III. John 8:12; 9:5: "I am the light of the world."

IV. John 10:7, 9: "I am the door of the sheep."

V. John 10:11, 14: "I am the good shepherd."

VI. John 11:25: "I am the resurrection and the life."

VII. John 14:6: "I am the way, the truth, and the life."

VIII. John 15:1: "I am the true vine."

IX. John 18:5: When the servants of the chief priests and Pharisees accompanying Judas came to arrest Jesus, He said, "I am" (the same as 8:58), pointing out His Messiahship.

It is worth noting that the Lord always used the present tense of the verb *eimí,* to be. This is the historic present implying that there never was, is, nor shall be a time that He has not been the bread of life, the light of the world, the door of the sheep (believers), the good shepherd, the resurrection and the life, the way, the truth and the life, the true vine, and the predestined lamb (*amnós* [286], the sacrificial lamb [John 1:29, 36; Acts 8:32; 1 Pet. 1:19]) of God.

Jesus Christ has always been the unique One through whom God reveals Himself, in a true relational way, as our Father. When Jesus Christ becomes our Lord, God indeed becomes our Father and we have access to Him, calling Him "our Father in heaven" (Matt. 6:9; John 1:12). If God is not our personal heavenly Father, it is because Jesus Christ has not become our Lord. Such a relationship is impossible for anyone who has many gods and many lords (1 Cor. 8:5). Seek the only Lord Jesus

Christ and accept His absolute rule. He will indwell you (Rom. 8:10), and so will the Father (1 John 4:12; 2 Cor. 6:16), and the Holy Spirit (John 14:16; James 4:5), and He will give you life that is more abundant (John 10:10).

The Lord Jesus Christ has an eternal relationship with the Father God (John 1:18). In the New Testament, God is presented as His Father. During His incarnate life, Jesus introduces God as "my Father in heaven" (Matt. 7:21; 10:32, 33; 12:50; 15:13; 16:17; 18:10, 19, 35).

"And one Lord *who is* Jesus Christ." Here the verb "is" must be implied. As there is "one" God the Father (the verb "is" is also implied here), unto us there is "one" Lord. Only God who is the Father exists and only one Lord who is Jesus Christ. If we were to imply the verb in the latter statement, it would read, "and there is one Lord who is Jesus Christ."

Jesus Christ is a historical person. There **is** one Lord; this one Lord **is** Jesus of history; Jesus **is** the Christ, the predicted anointed of God (Mark 14:61–64; Luke 24:21). Andrew was right, when meeting the historical Jesus, to say, "We have found the Messiah, which is, being interpreted, the Christ" (John 1:41). John reports that the woman who met the historical Jesus at the well said, "I know [*oída* {1492}, to perceive, intuitively know, recognize who the person is] the Messiah comes, which is called Christ: when He is come, He will tell us all things" (John 4:25). He had told her that she had been married to five husbands although He had never seen the woman before nor heard anything about her (John 4:16–18). On this alone, she perceived that Jesus was a man of God.

The heathen people of Corinth who worshiped many gods and many lords had no one to speak to them and reveal who the true God was. Jesus proved that He was the Christ through His death and resurrection. Christian apologetics are not based on dumb idols, but on Jesus, a historical personality who proved that

He was the Christ. He earned the right to be called "Lord" and to have His words be called the "Words of Truth."

Roman Emperors Claimed to Be Gods, but Only Jesus Christ Proved His Lordship

Caligula (Gaius Caesar, A.D. 12–41), Roman Emperor (A.D. 37–41), son of Germanicus, had ordered his statue to be erected in the Temple at Jerusalem and required that he should be worshiped as God. After plotting against the Roman Senate, he was assassinated in A.D. 41. Domitian, also, was called in official reports "our lord and god." He was a cruel tyrant who was Roman emperor from A.D. 81 until his death in A.D. 96.

Jesus, because He was the Christ, was Lord prior to His incarnation, death, and resurrection, and this He had proved to His contemporaries. Peter at Pentecost said in Acts 2:22, "You men of Israel, hear these words; Jesus of Nazareth, a man approved of God among you by miracles and wonders and signs, which God did by him in the midst of you, as you yourselves also know." The Jews viewed Jesus as a mere man of Nazareth. How did He prove Himself Lord? First, by His miracles. But miracles are not enough. Moses performed miracles, too (Acts 7:36), but he was only a prophet (Acts 7:37). The disciples were given the power of miracle working, but they were still only commissioned disciples. Only of Jesus of Nazareth is it said that He is the Lord, the Christ. He was divinity before He was born to Mary: "In the beginning was the Word." This answers the question as to His preexistence. Before there was any beginning the Word (*ho Lógos*), Christ, had been. Notice the distinctness of His personality: "And the Word was toward the God [the Father]." Christ in His eternal existence was a personality distinct from the Father, yet He was God: "And God was the Word" (John 1:1). We must understand that Christ who always had been God became incarnate. He did not achieve deity through His miracles. He performed miracles because He was God, and thus the miracles were in His own prerogative and power.

In speaking of Jesus, Peter said to the Jews on the day of Pentecost, "Him, being delivered by the determinate counsel and foreknowledge of God [the Father], you have taken, and by wicked hands have crucified and slain: whom God [the Father] has raised up, having loosed the pains of death: because it was not possible that He should be held by it" (Acts 2:23, 24). He was Lord of all before He became man, and He continues to be Lord. This is why He said, "I . . . have the keys of Hades and death" (Rev. 1:18). Jesus is unique. He was the Lord over death, but He was that before He became man, and He exercised this authority while He was the God-Man. Observe that He says, "I am the living One [*ho zṓn*: *ho*, the; *zṓn*, the present participle of *záō* {2198}, to live], and I became [*egenómēn*, the first person second aorist middle deponent of *gínomai*, to become] dead, and behold, I am living unto the ages of the ages," that is, forever (Rev. 1:18).

The Resurrection of Jesus Proved Him Lord

Jesus as the Son was coequal and coeternal with the Father from the beginning (John 1:18). In Acts 13:33 Paul quotes Psalm 2:7 and connects God's begetting of the Son with the Lord's resurrection: "that he resurrected Jesus; as it is also written in the second psalm, 'Thou art my Son, this day have I begotten thee.' " This is also quoted in Hebrews 1:5, and it definitely refers to the resurrection of Jesus as the entrance into a new and heavenly life where death has no more power (Rom. 1:4; Col. 1:18). The resurrection of Jesus is pivotal to the proof of His deity to human witnesses and to the distinction of the Father/Son relationship.

The Relationship of God the Father and God the Son

The Father is God and Father of the Lord Jesus Christ as 2 Corinthians 1:3 states: "Blessed [*eulogētós* {2128}, inherently praiseworthy] the God and Father of the Lord Jesus Christ, the Father of sympathies [*oiktirmṓn*, the genitive plural of *oiktirmós* {3628}] and God of all comfort."

Paul in Ephesians 1:17 further says: "That the God of our Lord Jesus Christ, the Father of glory [the Father of divine recognition] may give unto you [the] spirit of wisdom and revelation in the superknowledge [*epígnōsis* {1922}, knowledge that comes by faith] of Him [the Lord Jesus Christ]." This verse teaches us several important things:

I. He is not the Father of Christ in point of time and space, but forever. The verb "is" in the phrase is implied and therefore inserted. "The God [with the definite article thus meaning the Father {John 1:1}] of our Lord Jesus Christ, *who is* the Father of glory [*dóxa* {1391}, recognition of deity], may give you the spirit of wisdom [*sophía* {4678}, the ability to recognize what is divine] and [acceptable] revelation [*apokálupsis* {602}, revelation versus *anakálupsis*, discovery, or *anakalúptō* {343}, to discover] in the superknowledge of him." This eternal relationship of the Father and the Son is revealed from above and is not made by earthly discovery. How could it be otherwise since God is eternal and we are limited by time and space in everything? What is inconceivable by human thought must be divinely revealed if it is to be comprehended. One of the concepts is that of the Father being eternally the Father of the Lord Jesus Christ. How can one be the Father of another who is eternally Lord of all? Because they are equal, but both are God. "I and My Father are one [*hén*]" (John 10:30). They are one in essence, but distinct in personality. Our minds are too limited to fully comprehend that eternal relationship.

II. It takes the "spirit of wisdom" to understand such a relationship. The verb "may give you" is *dṓē*, the third person singular second aorist active subjunctive of the verb *dídōmi* (1325), to give. From this we may learn that:

A. The Spirit of God is the only way whereby we may be enabled to believe the existence of such an eternal relationship between God the Father and God the Son, or the Lord Jesus Christ.

B. Being in the aorist it means that we are given this ability to believe.

C. This ability to believe is entirely a gift of God as the verb explicitly states. The verb *dídōmi* means to give as a gift, not because we deserve it, but because of the character of the Giver.

The Gift of God

What is the gift of God that we all need in order to believe in this eternal relationship of the divine Persons? It is "spirit of wisdom." There is no definite article before the word *pneúma* (4151), spirit: ". . . that He may give you spirit of wisdom." Does Paul here speak of the Holy Spirit or of the spirit of man enlightened by the Holy Spirit? I believe it is the latter, as in Ephesians 1:18 he says, "The eyes of your heart [*dianoías*, understanding {TR, KJV}] being enlightened [*pephōtisménous*, the accusative plural perfect passive participle of *phōtízō* {5461}, to enlighten effectively] in order to perceive [*eidénai*, the perfect active infinitive of *oída*, from *eídō*, to perceive] what is the hope of his calling and what the riches of the glory of his inheritance in the saints."

This gift is in the realm of the spirit which is that part of man which the Holy Spirit enlightens. It enables a believer to put spiritual truth together and make it understandable to man's intelligence.

Paul in Colossians 2:2, 3 says something parallel which can help us accept the truth of the full assurance of our faith in what is revealed but not understood by the restricted mind of man: "That their hearts might be comforted, being knit together in love, and unto all riches of the full assurance of understanding, to the acknowledgment of the mystery of God, and of the Father, and of Christ. In whom are hid all the treasures of wisdom and knowledge."

The Mystery of God

What is "the mystery of God and the Father and of [the] Christ"? This mystery (*mustḗrion* [3466]) is a reality that cannot be known by investigation, a spiritual tenet which rests on revelation and cannot be understood in terms of human reason. In the New Testament, a mystery is a secret pertaining to matters of God's eternal purposes that have been or are being revealed.

Paul in Ephesians 3:3 confesses that this mystery was revealed to him: "How that by revelation he made known unto me the mystery." Revelation became personal knowledge.

In verse 4, Paul further states that the acceptance of such a revelation adds to our understanding. "Whereby, when you read, you may understand [*noḗsai*, the aorist active infinitive of *noéō* {3539}, to comprehend initially] my knowledge [*súnesin* {4907}, ability to understand concepts and see relationships between them; cf. Luke 2:47; 1 Cor. 1:19; Col. 1:9; 2:2; 2 Tim. 2:7] in the mystery of Christ." This means that the acceptance of the mystery of Christ, that He is Lord of all things and that there is one God the Father, does not stand counter to a man's intelligence.

And then in verse 5, "Which in other [*hetérais* {2087}, other but different than ours] ages [*geneaís*, the dative plural of *geneá* {1074}, generation] was not made known unto the sons of men, as it is now revealed unto his holy apostles and prophets by the Spirit."

This is an affirmation of the Trinity: God the Father, the mystery of Christ, and the Holy Spirit who is the Revealer of this relationship of the Father and the Son.

Now let us go back to Colossians 2:2, "That their hearts might be comforted, being knit together in love, and unto all riches of the full assurance of understanding [*súnesis,* the same word as in Eph. 3:4], to the acknowledgement [*epígnōsis*, superknowledge, knowledge that comes by faith as in Eph. 1:17] of the mystery of God, and of the Father, and of Christ." These two persons, God the Father and God the Son who has always been Lord, enlighten not only our understanding, but also bind our hearts in love. We become rich in knowledge and rich in love. This faith in having a common Father and Lord makes us new creatures capable of loving each other, for God is love (1 John 4:8, 16).

The Agent and Sustainer of Creation

The Lord Jesus in His eternal existence is the One "through whom all things are held together." The preposition used is not *ex* or *ek* (1537), of, as stated of the Father God, but *diá* (1223), through. "And one Lord Jesus Christ, **through** whom all things are held together." The Greek text does not have a verb. It could be "are" or "exist" or "hold together" (*sunéstēken*, the third person singular present perfect active indicative of *sunístēmi* [4921], to stand together). This is the verb used in Colossians 1:17 referring to the Lord Jesus Christ of whom it is said, "And he is before all things, and in [*en* {1722}, in or by] him all things consist [*sunéstēke*, have been holding together]."

This is the same preposition that is used in John 1:3: "All things came to be through [*diá*] him [the Logos who is God]."

The Lord Jesus Christ is the agent through whom the Father created all things and through whom the Father "holds together" everything. Electrons complete billions of trips around the nucleus of an atom in a millionth of a second. What keeps them from flying apart? Everything we know is made of atoms. What holds them all together? What holds two particles of hydrogen together with one particle of oxygen to make water? The Lord Jesus Christ. It is sad that people accept His composite gifts, but not the Giver.

He who sustains everything can only be God. And He is called that by Paul in Romans 9:5: "Whose are the fathers, and of whom as concerning the flesh Christ came, who is [*ho ṓn,* the One being, the present participle of *eimí,* to be] over all, God blessed forever. Amen." Peter in 2 Peter 1:1 affirms, "Simon Peter, a servant and an apostle of Jesus Christ, to them that have obtained like precious faith with us through the righteousness of God and our Savior Jesus Christ." Peter implies that He could not be our Savior if He were not God.

Believers Are What They Are Through Christ

"Yet to us" is the phrase with which this verse begins; "and we through [*diá*] him" is the phrase with which it closes. "And we" refers to Paul and all other believers. It speaks of what God and Jesus Christ are for the believers and what the believers are through Him. We come to the Father through the Son. "For there is one God, and one mediator between God and men, the man Christ Jesus" (1 Tim. 2:5). This is why Jesus Christ takes His position with God in the lives of believers. In this position, He exercises such functions as had been attributed to God and receives such reverence as had been accorded to God alone.

Prayer thus is addressed to Him (Acts 7:60; Rom. 10:9–12; 1 Cor. 1:2; 2 Cor. 12:8).

He will judge the world (Acts 17:31).

He is omniscient. (1 Cor. 4:5).

It is He who assigns various lots to men (1 Cor. 7:17); who grants power of service and endows with grace (1 Tim. 1:12, 14); who stands by and strengthens in times of trouble (2 Tim. 4:17), and delivers out of persecutions (2 Tim. 3:11).

All authority in the church should proceed from Him (1 Cor. 5:4; 2 Cor. 10:8; 13:10).

Baptism is to be performed in His name (Acts 8:16; 10:48).

He is not only the efficient agent of creation, but He is the creator of all things (Col. 1:16) and Lord over all beings (Acts 10:36; Rom. 10:12), our only Master and Lord (Jude 1:4).

But perhaps the most striking thing of all in the Christian consciousness of how Christ is God is the fact that quotations from the Old Testament which manifestly refer to God are immediately and repeatedly applied to Christ in the New Testament. For instance, the exhortation of the Psalmist to taste and see that the Lord is good (Ps. 34:8) is interpreted (1 Pet. 2:3) with reference to the believer experiencing the salvation of Jesus Christ.

Paul finds an answer to the question of Isaiah 40:13 (Sept.), "Who has known the mind of the Lord?" in the triumphant declaration, "But we have the mind of Christ" (1 Cor. 2:16, cf. Rom. 10:13; 1 Cor. 1:31; 10:22; 2 Cor. 3:16, 18; 10:17; 1 Pet. 3:15).

Acknowledgement of Christ's Lordship is presented by Paul as the mark of the true believer (Col. 2:6). To confess Him as Lord with one's mouth, and to believe in one's heart that God has raised Him from the dead (observe the connection between the resurrection and Lordship), is to be assured of salvation (Rom. 10:9). The proclamation of Christ's Lordship was the central theme of the apostle's preaching (2 Cor. 4:5) and the universal recognition of that Lordship, the consummation of the divine purpose.

LESSONS:

1. God is Father to the believer in Jesus Christ.
2. The doctrine of the Trinity is beyond human intelligence.
3. The Trinity is believable because it was revealed by Jesus Christ who proved Himself trustworthy through His predicted, realized, and attested resurrection.
4. The *'ᵉlōhīm* (God) of the Old Testament is the Trinity specified in the New Testament.
5. God is not only the creator, but the sustainer of all things (Col. 1:17).
6. The Trinity is active in the redemption of man. Jesus Christ saves the sinner, the Father receives the saved sinner, and the Holy Spirit makes it all possible.
7. All three Persons of the Trinity not only cooperate in the work of man's redemption, but all three indwell the believer. They enable him to live for God and to have victory over sin and life after death.
8. God rules as a Father in the believer's life when Jesus Christ becomes Lord and the Holy Spirit becomes the convicting power.
9. The resurrection of Jesus Christ is indisputable proof of His unique Lordship.
10. The spirit of wisdom is given to the believer so that he may accept with illumined intelligence what Jesus Christ revealed God to be: God the Father, God the Son, and God the Holy Spirit.

1 Cor. 8:7 | Do Your Actions Speak Louder Than Your Words?

*But this knowledge **is** not in all. But some, conscious of the idol, even now eat **realizing** it is meat sacrificed to idols, and their conscience, being weak, is defiled."*

The apostle Paul here begins this verse with the adversative particle *allá* (235), but. This is the second "but" in this chapter. The first one is in verse 6 where the apostle contrasts the believers in the one true God with those who sacrifice to idols. Now in verse 7, "but" stands in contrast to the statement in verse 1 that "We perceive that we all have knowledge." It was a general knowledge that animals were sacrificed to idols which were considered as gods and lords even though they had no real existence.

The knowledge of which the apostle now speaks in verse 7 is the full knowledge of what was going on in the sacrifice of animals to idols and the disposal of the carcasses that were left over. Although it was general knowledge that animals were sacrificed to idols, it was impossible for anyone to know the full situation of each individual who was partaking of any of that meat. The "not" in the statement "but this knowledge is not in all" is the absolute negative *ou* (3756) indicating that there is absolutely no one in whom the full knowledge of the situation is present.

"In all" is *en* (1722), in; *pásin*, the dative plural masculine adjective of *pás* (3956), all, or in each person. There are some who constitute an exception, who know that although sacrifices are offered to idols yet they are nonentities—they are not God (v. 4). Therefore, they eat in full conscience of the fact that they are not sinful by eating, and there can be no absolute position on any one conviction. It is a matter of one's own conscience, since there is no authoritative rule whereby the act of eating or not eating can be judged.

Specific Knowledge Is Referred to Here

The word "knowledge" here has the definite article in front of it, unlike the first mention of the word "knowledge" (*gnṓsis* [1108]) in verse 1. Paul states in that verse that we perceive that we all have knowledge that animals were sacrificed to idols. But this knowledge (*hē* [3588], the feminine article preceding *gnṓsis*) refers to the fact that idols are nonentities (v. 4).

Why Some Ate Meat Sacrificed to Idols

"But some, conscious of the idol, even now eat realizing that it is meat sacrificed to idols." Here the apostle Paul is describing the Christians who knew what they were doing. In their conscience they knew that the meat was sacrificed to an idol, but they still ate it. And this they did further realizing that the idols to which they were sacrificing were nothing in the world (v. 4).

What should the attitude of other Christians be toward those Christians in Corinth who ate meat sacrificed to idols against their own conscience? We should only judge them as if they did not have full knowledge of the matter. "But some with conscience of the idol unto this hour eat [it] as a thing offered to idols." "But some" is *tinés dé* (*tinés*, the nominative plural masculine indefinite pronoun *tís* [5101], someone; *dé* {1161}, but).

The TR and the MT have *tḗ suneidḗsei*, with the conscience, the dative feminine of *suneídēsis* (4893), conscience. This means that they were eating these meats with a clear conscience. A question arises as to whether the word is *suneídēsis*, conscience, or *sunḗtheía* (4914), custom, habit. The KJV translates the word as "conscience" which is found in the TR and MT, while the other critical texts have *tḗ sunḗtheía*, according to custom. The expression *tē senḗtheía* does not occur anywhere else in the New Testament, while *tḗ suneidḗsei* is used by the apostle Paul in Acts 23:1; 1 Timothy 3:9 and 2 Timothy 1:3. The word "conscience" occurs 20 times in the epistles of Paul while the word *sunḗtheia*, custom, occurs only twice in all the New Testament (John 18:39; 1 Cor. 11:16). Although the modern translations have opted for "custom," I opt to take the word as being "conscience" here. The meaning, therefore, is that some in whom there was the full knowledge of the matter ate of the meat sacrificed to idols without a condemning conscience.

What Is Conscience?

The first thing that we need to examine is the meaning of the word "conscience" (*suneídēsis*). It is a compound word made up of the preposition *sún* (4862), with or together, and having the particular meaning of conjointly, and the verb *eídō* (1492), to perceive, to know intuitively. Conscience constitutes the moral consciousness that something is right or wrong. It implies the intuitive knowledge that something that we choose to do is either in agreement with or contrary to the law of the knowledge of good and evil that God has placed in our hearts. It is that God-given inner apprehension of moral truth. The apostle Paul in Romans 2:15 equates conscience with the work of the law. What the law designates as moral, the conscience, which is an inbuilt characteristic of man having been made in the image of

God, innately confirms or objects to its permissibility. That is to say, it confronts man when he transgresses the law of God. A man who kills another man cannot plead ignorance of the law which says, "Thou shalt not kill," because he has an innate knowledge as a human being that murder is wrong. Conscience, therefore, is that which Paul designates as the moral faculty that God has designed into human nature. (See the book *Conscience* on Luke 11:33–36.)

The Moral Perception of the Conscience Depends on What One Is and How He Has Been Instructed

Humanity is divided into two parts, the unredeemed and those restored and redeemed by Christ. The knowledge of those who are redeemed in Christ is much greater insofar as moral conduct is concerned. That is why the conscience of the believer is instructed by the law given by God which is alive in his heart in addition to that inherent ability of discernment of moral conduct. In Romans 2:18 the apostle Paul gives us an inkling of how God instructed first the conscience of the Jews versus that of the heathen: "And you know [*ginṓskeis*, the second person singular present active indicative of *ginṓskō* {1097}, to experientially know] **His** [in the original there is the accusative singular neuter article *tó*] will [*thélēma* {2307} indicating that God's will is made known to each individual by God Himself] and you approve [*dokimázeis*, the second person singular present active indicative of *dokimázō* {1381}, to test, prove, distinguish] the things that are different one from the other [*diaphéronta*, the accusative plural neuter present active participle of *diaphérō* {1308} from *diá* {1223}, denoting transition or separation, and *phérō* {5342}, to carry, bear], being instructed [*katēchoúmenos*, the nominative singular present passive participle of *katēchéō* {2727}, to catechize, indoctrinate, instruct, inform] out of the law." It indicates that things are different one from the other, and they must be distinguished as to their moral impact on individuals by instruction from the law. This verse was specifically addressed to Jews, and it tells them that the law was given to sharpen their conscience. This is why a Jew takes the law which God gave in the Old Testament as the refinement of that inner voice given to all people called conscience. From this verse we learn that the individual is to decide for himself what is moral and what is not according to the specific instructions of God in view of the opportunities He has provided for him.

There is another basic truth, however, that can be derived from this. It is that the moral faculty of man known as conscience by itself is an inadequate moral guide (Jer. 17:9). The conscience of the Jew may be different than the conscience of the heathen, and the conscience of a redeemed Christian is different still.

The Training and Freedom of the Christian Conscience

The training of the human conscience is progressive. Man in his degenerate state has only the unwritten law of moral conscience to guide him, while the Jews have in addition the Law of Moses, and the Christians have Christ within their hearts who is the fulfillment of the law (Matt. 5:17–20; Rom. 8:7; Phil. 1:21).

Even those who have Christ indwelling them may display differences in judgment concerning things which pertain to matters of individual discernment which they must make as they live the Christian life. There is a theological term that has been coined to designate those things that are to be decided by the Christian conscience as it is instructed by Christ. It is the term *adiáphora*, the nonessentials, things that make no difference, or are of minor importance.

Some of the explicit commands of Paul in 1 Corinthians are indicated by the imperative, "flee" (*pheúgete*, the second person plural present active imperative of *pheúgō* [5343], to escape, run away from). He uses this command in 1 Corinthians 6:18 when he says, "Flee fornication. Every sin that a man does is without the body; but he who commits fornication sins against his own body." And in 1 Corinthians 10:14, Paul says, "Flee from idolatry." These are explicit commands of the Word of God.

But the question as to whether Christians ought to eat only vegetables and fruit or include meat in their diets pertains to the realm of *adiáphora*, the things which are of minor importance to the Christian faith no matter what one chooses to do. For instance, is one a better Christian if he is a vegetarian, and is he a better Christian if he prefers to eat beef and lamb, but not pork? Jewish believers may feel uncomfortable eating pork; Indian believers may prefer not to eat beef. Who are we to judge them? These are the difficult determinations which each believer himself is permitted to make according to the instruction that his conscience has had. For as Paul says in 1 Corinthians 8:8, "But meat does not commend us to God: for neither if we eat, are we the better; neither if we eat not, are we the worse."

What Is a Weak Conscience?

Here in 1 Corinthians 8:7 Paul speaks of the conscience of the believers being weak (*asthenḗs* [772] derived from the privative alpha, *a*–[1], without, and *sthénos*, strength, and the verb *sthenóō* [4599], to strengthen). Therefore, the conscience can be strong or weak and there are certain behaviors of the Christian life that show the health of the Christian conscience.

It is to be noted that of the 30 times that the word "conscience" (*suneídēsis*) is used in the New Testament, 22 times it is used by the apostle Paul (Acts 23:1; 24:16; Rom. 2:15; 9:1;

13:5; 1 Cor. 8:7, 10, 12; 10:25, 27, 28, 29 [twice]; 2 Cor. 1:12; 4:2; 5:11; 1 Tim. 1:5, 19; 3:9; 4:2; 2 Tim. 1:3; Titus 1:15); five times it is used in the book of Hebrews (9:9, 14; 10:2, 22; 13:18); and three times by Peter (1 Pet. 2:19; 3:16, 21). In the two chapters in which Paul is dealing with the matter of eating meats sacrificed to idols, he refers eight times to the conscience (1 Cor. 8:7, 10, 12; 10:25, 27, 28, 29 [twice]). In all three of the occurrences in chapter 8, he speaks of the weak conscience, and in verse 7 we are given to understand what the weak conscience is. A weak conscience is one that is uncertain as to whether something is sinful or not, or that considers something to be sinful which is in fact not sinful. Hence, a Christian with a weak conscience who has spent his or her life worshiping idols and associating such meat with the idols to whom it was offered may feel that it is sinful to purchase and eat that meat. Paul affirms in verse 8 that there is no sin in partaking of the meat, but in verses 9 and 12 warns that we sin if we let our liberty of conscience become a stumblingblock to a brother with a weak conscience.

"But not in all is there this knowledge." This means that not all have the full knowledge that these meats which they have been eating are possibly meats sacrificed to idols. On the other hand, there are some that do. This is indicated by *tinés,* the nominative plural masculine indefinite pronoun of *tís* (5101), someone, and *dé*, but. "But some" of the following phrase stands in contrast to *pásin*, the dative plural masculine adjective of *pás*, all. Not in all is there the knowledge that what they are eating has been sacrificed to idols, whereas in some there is the consciousness that it has been but they know that idols are nothing in the world (v. 4). Their conscience, therefore, does not condemn them.

But some eat being conscious that the meat has been sacrificed to idols. They eat (*esthíousin*, the third person plural present active indicative of *esthíō* [2068], to eat) even until now, until the present time. This is expressed by *héōs* (2193), until, and *árti* (737), now, to this present time. This means that they were eating these meats when they were idolaters, before they became Christians, and even now after they have become Christians they continue to eat them. There has been no discontinuation of their custom. It is their belief about idols which has changed. Maybe this is why some texts have substituted the word *suneidḗsei*, conscience, with the word *sunētheía*, custom. Their conversion to Christianity has not made them discontinue eating meats sacrificed to idols. But why? Because their conviction about idols is now different.

Former Habits Carried Over Into the Christian Life Ought to be Scrutinized

When a person is converted, his or her lifestyle has to be examined, not only in how each custom affects oneself, but also others in the faith and out of the faith, and whether it glorifies God or brings shame to Him. When we are born again, the customs of the old man do not rule our life, and the conscience becomes sensitized. The Christian needs to examine whether there are explicit prohibitions in the Word of God concerning the customs of one's past lifestyle. If there are any such as fornication or idolatry (1 Cor. 6:18; 10:14), the believer must immediately flee from them. But there are innumerable details that must be examined by one's own conscience as it is illumined by the light of Christ that is now shining in his or her heart. In the matter of partaking of meats sacrificed to idols, there are new considerations. The believer in Christ now, not being an idolater, realizes that idols are nothing in the world (v. 4). Before he ate as a matter of custom. Now he eats realizing the truth about idols being nonentities, and his freedom to participate is a matter of conviction.

But the question that arises is not merely how things permitted by an informed and enlightened conscience are going to be enjoyed by oneself, but how they are going to affect the lives of others whose conscience is not as well informed. This is what Paul calls a weak conscience.

The last part of the verse states, "And their conscience, being weak, is defiled." Paul in Romans 14 deals with those who are weak in the faith (v. 1). They should not be despised (*exouthenéō* [1848]) by those whose informed conscience permits them to eat everything permissible (vv. 2–5). The example we provide to others is essential in our attitude regarding nonessentials of life. Although we may be fully informed about our faith, we should not disregard our fellow travelers in this life.

What is translated "is defiled" is *molúnetai*, the third person singular present middle/passive indicative of *molúnō* (3435), to defile, soil as with mud or filth, found only here in 1 Corinthians 8:7 and in Revelation 3:4 and 14:4. The conscience of the believer who does not care how others feel about his own actions will grow callous. This is what Scripture calls blindness, callousness, hardness, insensitivity (*pṓrōsis* [4457] and *pōróō* [4458], to defile, become spiritually and morally insensitive; Mark 3:5; Rom. 11:7; 2 Cor. 3:14; Eph. 4:18).

The Necessity of the Constant Cleansing of the Conscience

The opposite of "to defile" is "to cleanse" (*katharízō* [2511]). In Hebrews 9:14 the apostle speaks of the necessity of purging our conscience with the same blood of the Lord Jesus Christ which we claimed for salvation. "How much more shall the blood of Christ, who through the eternal Spirit offered himself without spot to God, purge [*kathariei*, the third person singular future active indicative of *katharízō*] your conscience from dead works to serve the living God?" This indicates that though our hearts have been cleansed by the blood of Christ once and for all and we are attached to the body of Christ (1 Cor. 12:13), still our conscience needs to be cleansed continuously in our Christian life. Therefore, our conscience, after our regeneration, can be defiled or cleansed by what we do. It will become defiled if we do not constantly allow the blood of Christ to convict us and cleanse us from the old practices of our sinful life. One of the ways to cleanse our own conscience is by not doing anything to defile the conscience of a weak brother or sister in the faith (Rom. 14:1).

Paul, in writing to youthful Timothy, was eager for the cleansing of the conscience to be accomplished in Timothy's young heart. That is why Paul admonishes him in 1 Timothy 1:5: "Now the end of the commandment is charity out of a pure heart, and of a good conscience, and of faith unfeigned." The Christian should demonstrate love from a pure heart and benevolent (*agathḗs* [18]) conscience. How is one's conscience cleansed? Not by thinking of oneself alone, but of others, too. The attitude that what we are doing is our own business and does us no harm is sinful. We must consider whether or not our actions edify both ourselves and others. Our attitude must be positive.

In 1 Timothy 1:19 Paul says, "Holding faith, and a good [*agathḗn*] conscience; which some having put away concerning faith have made shipwreck." In 1 Timothy 3:9 Paul says, "Holding the mystery of the faith in a pure [*kathará* {2513}, clean, pure] conscience."

In 1 Timothy 4:2, referring to false prophets, Paul speaks of them as having their conscience seared. These are described as those who pretend to have faith but really do not. Their false faith makes them extremists in demanding behavior such as "forbidding to marry and commanding to abstain from meats, which God has created to be received with thanksgiving of them which believe and know the truth" (v. 3). Paul argues that we are free to eat all kinds of food, but we must, at the same time, remember that "meat commends us not to God, for neither if we eat, are we the better; neither, if we eat not, are we the worse" (1 Cor. 8:8). Again, we come to the matter of influencing others and not to the absolute right that we have to enjoy anything and everything without respect to their conscience.

In 2 Timothy 1:3 Paul writes, "I thank God, whom I serve from my forefathers with pure conscience, that without ceasing I have remembrance of you in my prayers night and day." This indicates that Paul constantly examined his conscience to see whether it was pure, as we must also.

In Titus 1:15 Paul tells us, "Unto the pure all things are pure, but unto those who are defiled [*memiasmémois*, the dative plural masculine perfect passive participle of *miaínō* {3392}, to pollute, defile, the synonym of *molúnō*; however the former signifies ceremonial defilement while the latter refers to moral defilement] and unbelieving, nothing is pure; but even their mind and conscience is defiled [*memíantai*, the third person singular perfect passive indicative of *miaínō*]."

LESSONS:

1. There is an explicit moral code of Christian conduct which we are enabled to follow through our new birth. We know, for instance, that we should flee from fornication (1 Cor. 6:18) and from idolatry (1 Cor. 10:14). A person who is a fornicator or an idolater cannot, at the same time, be a believer in Jesus Christ.
2. There are, however, in our Christian lives, behaviors that can characterize us as strong or weak, without affecting our eternal relationship with Christ.
3. The carry-over habits of the old life can characterize us as having a weak conscience.

4. The submission to such a weak conscience of the Christian life is a defilement to our Christian conscience which ought to be diligently cleansed by the blood of Christ.
5. The duty of the Christian is not to do merely what he has the right to do, but what he ought to do in view of his brethren lest he become a stumblingblock to them.
6. The question to ask in choosing conduct is not whether I can do certain things without risking my eternal salvation, but whether these things will build me and others up in the Christian faith.

1 Cor. 8:8 — Food Neither Commends Nor Condemns Us to God

Nevertheless, food does not commend us to God; nor if we were to eat would we count for more, nor if we were not to eat would we lack."

Evidently there were two categories of Christian believers in Corinth: those who ate meats sacrificed to idols without any compunction of the weaker brother's conscience; and those who did not eat any of the meat sacrificed to idols, even if it was cheaper, because of concession to the weaker brother's conscience. It seems, however, that the latter criticized the former. This is what led the apostle Paul to lay down the general principle that the food we eat or do not eat, as long as it is not knowingly harmful, does not in itself commend us to God nor does it indicate or affect our relationship with God. Such a relationship is determined by our spirit.

What Does Commend Us to God?

In 1 Corinthians 8:4 we have the noun *brōsis* (1035), the act of eating, and in this verse we have the noun *brōma* (1033), which is the actual food consumed. "Food does not commend us to God." The negative here is expressed by the word *ou* (3756), not, which is absolute in its meaning. The verb is *parístēsi,* the present active indicative of *parístēmi* (3936) which is derived from *pará*

(3844), near, and *hístēmi* (2476), to place, stand. It means that food does not cause us to stand near or place us near to God to be commended by Him. If food could achieve a good relationship with God, we had better find which food does and use it. No food, however, will bring a good relationship with God. Nor will those, seeing what we eat, be able to determine whether our relationship with God is good or bad. Very clearly, Paul in Romans 14:17 states: "For the kingdom of God is not meat and drink [*brṓsis*, the act of eating; *pósis* {4213}, the act of drinking], but righteousness [*dikaiosúnē* {1343}, righteousness which is conformity to all that He commands or appoints, rendering to God and to our fellow human beings their proper rights] and peace [*eirḗnē* {1515}, peace as a state given by Jesus Christ, tranquility {John 16:33}] and joy in the Holy Spirit." In other words, Paul declares here that what one eats does not qualify him for the kingdom of God, nor can it do in the human heart what only faith can do. It is the clean heart, and not clean food, that will matter at the end. The weak brother should be careful not to defile his conscience. And if another is weak in seeing the truth regarding a particular issue, do not confuse him by eating certain foods claiming you have the right to do so without due consideration of how your conduct will affect him.

The tense of the verb *parístēmi*, to commend, in the TR and the MT, is the present indicative *parístēsi*, commends us to God. In the United Bible Society and the Critical Text it is *parastḗsei*, the third person future active indicative meaning, "It shall in no way commend us," referring to the time of the judgment seat of Christ (2 Cor. 5:10). I prefer the present tense *parístēsi*, indicating that food never does commend us to God at any time.

To Eat or Not to Eat

Then follows two suppositional phrases of reality: "neither **if** [*eán* {1437}] we eat do we count for more, nor **if** we do not eat do we lack." It is possible to have believers on either side of the spectrum, and no one should attempt to judge whether they are good or not-so-good Christians. Both sentences begin with the conjunction *oúte* (3777) derived from *ou*, the absolute negative, and the enclitic *te* (5037) meaning "and." What others eat should not lead us to an absolute judgment as to their spiritual standing. The two contrasting conditions are expressed with the verbs *perisseúomem*, the first person plural present active indicative of *perisseúō* (4052), to abound (in my duty as a believer), and the contrasting verb *husteroúmetha*, the first person plural present passive indicative of *husteréō* (5302), to be last, behind, posterior in place (figuratively of spiritual standing).

Our Lord's teaching on the subject is contained in a parabolic saying in Mark 7:15: "There is nothing from without a man that entering into him can defile him, but the things which come out of him, those are they that defile the man." When the disciples asked Him for further elucidation concerning this parable, He said, "Do you not perceive, that whatever thing from without that enters into the man, it cannot defile him; because it enters not into his heart but into the belly, and goes out in the discharge [*aphedrṓn* {856}, toilet], purging all meats?" (Mark 7:18, 19). The expression "purging all meats" has the word "meats" translated from *brṓmata*, the plural of *brṓma*, referring to the foods that were declared unclean by the Jews. Anyone who ate these foods was considered defiled. In conclusion, the Lord said "That which comes out of the man, that defiles the man. For from within, out of the heart of men, proceed evil thoughts, adulteries, fornications, murders, thefts, covetousness, wickedness, deceit, lasciviousness, an evil eye, blasphemy, pride, foolishness: all these things come from within and defile the man" (Mark 7:20–23).

In the selection of the food that we as Christians eat, we should not consider only ourselves and our relationship with the Lord. Equally important is the influence that our example will leave on other Christians, especially those with a weak conscience. Those who have an informed conscience and know that the food we eat does not commend us or steal away from our personal standing with God will understand our actions. But the question is what will happen to the conscience of a weak brother or a brother who is uninformed concerning a certain matter.

"All Things Are Not Expedient"

In the consideration of nonessential things, things that in themselves do not matter and for which there is no explicit direction in the Word of God, what should our decision be? While it is true that all things are permissible, should the believer consider only himself in the matter? What one considers personally permissible may not be beneficial to all, especially to the weak brethren. This thought is expressed in 1 Corinthians 6:12 and 10:23 and translated: "all things are not expedient." The word "expedient" is the translation of the Greek word *sumphérei*, the third person singular present active indicative of *sumphérō* (4851) derived from *sún* (4862), together conjointly, and *phérō* (5342), to bring. The impersonal verb means it was not to the common advantage or commonly profitable. As far as an individual believer was concerned, when he bought meat that was sacrificed to an idol, he may have saved money, for it was usually cheaper than other meat. Why should he not since the actual eating of that meat did not commend nor take away from his standing with God? But was he to consider only himself in this case?

This same reasoning is given by the apostle Paul in regard to circumcision. He says in 1 Corinthians 7:19, "Circumcision is nothing, and uncircumcision is nothing, but the keeping of the commandments of God" (cf. Gal. 5:6; 6:15). Being circumcised does not bring one any closer to God and not being circumcised does not detract anything from one's relationship with God.

The apostle Paul elaborates on this subject of individual freedom of the conscience in Romans 14:2–4 when he says,

> For one believes that he may eat all things: another, who is weak, eats herbs. Let not him who eats despise him who does not eat; and do not let him who eats not judge him who eats: for God has received him. Who are you that you judge another man's servant? To his own master he stands or falls. Yes, he will be upheld, for the master is able to make him stand.

And then in verses 5 and 6, Paul enlarges his argument to the Sabbath day and other holidays and their keeping. He says,

> One man esteems one day above another; another esteems every day alike. Let every man be fully persuaded in his own mind. He who regards the day, regards it unto the Lord, and he who regards not the day, to the Lord he does not regard it. He who eats, eats to the Lord, for he gives God thanks; and he who eats not, to the Lord he eats not, and gives God thanks.

And then follows the master statement: "For none of us lives to himself, and no man dies to himself" (Rom. 14:7).

In other words, there are others to consider besides oneself when deciding whether to do or not to do something, to eat or not to eat. In verse 12 Paul says, "So then each one [*hékastos* {1538}, each one individually] of us shall give account of himself to God."

LESSONS:

1. What foods we choose to eat or not eat do not affect our standing before God.
2. Abstaining from certain foods does not mean that we are walking close to the Lord.
3. The one who so abstains from certain foods should not be critical of the one who eats them.
4. There is a personal, individual accounting we shall give to the Lord concerning our behavior; nevertheless, we are responsible for the example we bear to others (1 Cor. 8:12, 13).

1 Cor. 8:9	***Do Not Let Your Freedom Become a Stumblingblock***

Be careful, however, lest perhaps in any way the exercise of your freedom does not become a stumblingblock to the weak.

When I choose to eat or not to eat certain foods, to keep a holiday or not to, to be benevolent on the day that I am to rest, it is not enough to consider my rights in these areas, but I must also consider how the exercise of these rights will affect others, especially those who are weak.

Just How Far Does Our Freedom Go?

In the *Daily Bread* published by the Radio Bible Class, there is the following devotional for October 29, 1959 which illustrates perfectly what the apostle Paul is saying in this verse:

> I don't see any harm in what I am doing, and therefore it is nobody's business but my own!" Have you ever heard anyone say that—or said it yourself? You indulge some habit which you feel is harmless in itself, but forget what effect it may have on someone else.
>
> A man was entertaining some children by lighting a match, and then placing the burning end in his mouth and extinguishing it. The father of one of the children seeing it, said, "I wish you would not do that, it is dangerous." The man replied, "I am not hurting myself." The reply was quick, "But it may hurt someone else." Then he pointed to his little

> son with a dressing on his upper lip. He said, "Yesterday my little Jimmy saw you do this trick, and he thought it was all right for him to try. See the result? He not only burned his lip but set fire to the tablecloth, and we barely kept the flames from spreading. You may not hurt yourself, but you have caused someone else to get hurt by your example.

As I was preparing this manuscript, there was a discussion on the newscast regarding the effect violence on television has on people, and especially children. One illustration given was that of two cartoon characters playing with fire. "Fire is fun," said one of them as he set a fire. A five-year-old child who watched the program set fire to his baby sister who died from the burns. The house also burnt down. While we might expect cartoon characters to behave irresponsibly since they are brainless, those who write the script should be responsible.

One of the things that the true Christian becomes is free in Christ. Jesus' discussion with the Pharisees became heated when he told them that they were slaves and needed to be freed (John 8:33). He concluded His discussion with them by saying, "If the Son therefore shall make you free, you shall be free indeed" (John 8:36). The Pharisees were slaves of sin (Rom. 6:17, 20; John 8:34). Christ frees the believer from the slavery of sin. "Being then made free from sin, you became the servants of righteousness" (Rom. 6:18). "But now, being made free from sin and having become servants to God, you have your fruit unto holiness, and the end everlasting life" (Rom. 6:22). This freedom, however, is freedom not to do whatever a man wants, but to do what the Spirit of God who indwells him wants (1 Cor. 6:19).

Restraint to Our Freedom

"Be careful, however, lest . . . ." There is an innate restraint to our God-given liberty here on earth. The first basic restraint is given to us by the cross of Christ (Rom. 6:6). The sin of Adam, however, left its impact upon us, and especially upon our bodies which are yet to be redeemed in the future (Rom. 8:23). This is why our bodies, although our souls are redeemed, are still subject to corruptibility, sickness, and death. Although they are redeemed from sin, the possibility of sinful acts remains in us and with us. For this reason, in Colossians 3:5, 6, we are called upon to mortify the members of our bodies: "Mortify, therefore, your members which are upon the earth; fornication, uncleanness, inordinate affection, evil concupiscence, and covetousness, which is idolatry for which things' sake the wrath of God comes on the children of disobedience."

On the one hand, we are admonished to "stand fast in the liberty wherewith Christ has made us free, and be not entangled again with the yoke of bondage" (Gal. 5:1); and on the other hand, we are cautioned not to allow our freedom in Christ to be misused in doing that which we can do but which serves selfish purposes. That is the meaning of the imperative *blépete*, be careful, watch it, here in 1 Corinthians 8:9. This is the second person plural present active imperative of the verb *blépō* (991), look to it, take heed, be on the watch, beware. We are told, however, in Ephesians 6:11 to "Put on the whole armor of God, that you may be able to stand against the wiles of the devil." And then in conclusion the apostle Paul says, "Stand, therefore, having your loins girded about with truth, and having on the breastplate of righteousness" (v. 6:14). We are cautioned "having been called to liberty" not to use our liberty for occasion of the flesh, but by love to serve one another (Gal. 5:13). We are told that we must be careful how we use this liberty that we have in Christ lest it be a stumblingblock to our brother (1 Cor. 8:11–13). Faith must always be guided by love. While faith in God through Jesus Christ has liberated us, that liberty should not be used indiscriminately but in love for others with whom we live. None of us lives unto himself or dies unto himself (Rom. 14:7).

This is why the apostle Paul in 1 Corinthians 8:9 has the adversative particle after the imperative verb *blépete*, be careful, watch out, but enjoy your freedom. Stand up for the fact that you can do anything, **but** (*dé* [1161]) make sure it is that which pleases Christ who has given you this liberty (Gal. 5:1).

The Greeks had always believed that freedom should have its own voluntary limitations, and they had a word to express this; it was *sōphrosúnē* (Acts 26:25; 1 Tim. 2:9, 15). This word actually means a sound mind. It is made up of the words *soâos,* from which the verb *soâzō* (4982), to save, is derived, and *phrónēsis* (5428), mind, prudence, the ability to govern one's own life wisely. This latter word *phrónēsis* is derived from *phreân* (5424), understanding, the brake that one applies by his mind to his fleshly desires. This is the ability to crucify the flesh which, Christ having done on the cross on our behalf, the believer is asked to do daily. "And they that are Christ's have crucified the flesh with the affections and lusts. If we live in the Spirit, let us also walk in the Spirit" (Gal. 5:24, 25). It is to believers, therefore, that Paul writes, "Be careful, however," or "But be careful."

The next two words, *mḗ* (3378), the relative "no" or "not," and *pōs* (4458), the enclitic particle of indefiniteness of manner, mean "in some way or other." We have translated it "lest perhaps in any way" to make the English text less confusing. When the two Greek words, *mḗ* and *pōs,* are used together making the one word *mḗpōs* (3381), it means so that, lest perhaps, by any means or in whatever way. This is the restraint that we should exercise in our freedom in Christ as we consider the influence we bear in society in general, among both believers and unbelievers.

A Christian's Authority in Determining His Conduct

"The exercise of your freedom." This word *exousía* (1849), permission, authority, right, liberty, power to act, needs to be carefully examined. The first thing we observe is that it is related to *éxesti* found in 1 Corinthians 6:12 and 10:23 which is the impersonal verb translated "It is permissible." Therefore, the noun of the verb *éxestin* is *exousía* which can be translated, "the right and the power to do that which I am able and I choose to do." The words *éxesti* and *exousía* combine the two ideas of right and might. As far as right, authority, or capacity is concerned, it involves ability, power, and strength. *Exousía* is the right which God has to do anything He wants in relation to nature (Rev. 14:18). This He gives restrictedly to natural forces (Rev. 6:8; 9:3, 10, 19; 16:9; 18:1). Also, He allows Satan to act only within a limited dominion (Luke 4:6; 22:53; Acts 26:18; Col. 1:13; Rev. 13:5, 7). Christ, in His status as the God-Man on earth, has **all** authority given to Him in heaven and on earth by the Triune God (Matt. 28:18). The historical Jesus claimed *exousía* to forgive sins (Mark 2:10), to expel demons (Mark 3:15), and to teach (Matt. 7:29; Mark 11:28; Luke 4:36). Insofar as the church is concerned, it derives its authority from Christ. Believers in turn receive their right as such from Him (John 1:12; Rev. 22:14). The Lord gave the apostles their authority (Matt. 10:1–8); hence they had to use it responsibly (cf. Mark 13:34; 1 Cor. 9:4ff.). Paul relates the *exousía* which he has to two principles, first what is proper and fitting and, second, its edification or effect on others. Therefore, *exousía* is not the freedom to use the power that we have from God as we want, but as the Holy Spirit who indwells us dictates (1 Cor. 6:19).

". . . lest perhaps in any way the exercise of your freedom does not become a stumblingblock to the weak." Here Paul describes the Spirit-imposed limitations of the authority which the believer has from Christ. This authority must be interpreted as the freedom to choose the action that demonstrates love and shows concern for the edification of self and others. But alongside the Greek word *exousía*, authority, right and might, stands the word *próskomma* (4348), a stumblingblock. It derives from the verb *proskóptō* (4350), to stumble. This, in turn, is derived from the preposition *prós* (4314), to, against, and *kóptō* (2875), to cut, strike. In the New Testament *próskomma* is that which others can stumble against, a stumblingblock. Figuratively, it is a cause of falling, an occasion of sinning (Rom. 14:13, 20; 1 Cor. 8:9). We who are strong in the faith should be careful in the exercise of our freedom or of our rights that we do not become a stumblingblock, especially to the weak (*toís asthenoúsin*, the dative plural masculine present active participle of *asthenéō* [770], without strength, power). The word is used here as a present participle, and refers to those who demonstrate that they are spiritually sick or without spiritual strength. They are presented as facing a spiritual decision and struggle. In this instance, they do not know whether to eat or not eat of the meat sacrificed to idols (v. 1). The question which we, the strong in the faith, should ask is, how is this going to affect others as they see us partake of it.

Stumblingblocks

To place a stumblingblock before a struggling believer is the same as offending or scandalizing him. The Greek word that can be taken as synonymous with *próskomma* in the New Testament is *skándalon* (4625), a triggered trap, a snare, offense (Rom. 14:13). The verb is *skandalízō* (4624), to entrap, trip up, entice. Our Lord in Matthew 18:6 spoke very definitely of not scandalizing one of the least of these, referring to those who were new in the faith. He equated them with little children, saying,

"But whoso shall offend one of these little ones which believe in me [*pisteuóntōn*, the genitive plural masculine present active participle of *pisteúō* {4100} which means those believing], it would be better for him that a millstone were hanged about his neck, and that he were drowned in the depths of the sea." Our concern then should not be primarily with our appearance before those who are well established in the faith, but those who are weak, those whom we are trying to establish in the faith. We should be concerned as to how our example is going to affect little children, so to speak.

The tense of the verb translated "become" should be noted. In Greek it is *génētai*, the third person singular aorist middle deponent subjunctive of *gínomai* (1096), to become. The aorist subjunctive indicates "to become" at a particular time as a result of a particular choice one makes in the exercise of his freedom in Christ. What influence or effect will our every action have on little ones, whether they are children in age or only children in the faith? How wonderful it would be if, before every action in the exercise of the authority we have been given, we were to ask ourselves this question? *The Upper Room* of May 13, 1964 provided the following illustration:

> Sometimes the smallest stream will change its course. The alteration may be due to no visible obstacle. But on closer examination, we may discover that a rock or the stump of a tree, hidden from view by the rushing waters, has silently changed the course of that stream.
>
> Thus every person has influence—for good or for evil. The Christian faith puts the responsibility upon the individual for his own actions, as well as its influence upon his fellow man.
>
> All too often we fail to recognize, or ignore the fact, that our actions and influences are observed and felt without our being aware of it. Are those affected by our influence made better or worse by it?

If what I do would hurt someone else, it is wrong—even though it may not harm me. Paul saw no harm in eating meat offered to idols, but was willing to forego this right if it injured his testimony. This is also the Christian principle to be applied to our entire conduct. Someone has written wisely, "Every Christian must be very watchful for those occasions when he should deny himself certain tastes and habits which are often harmful to others. For their sake, we will abstain." Conspicuous illustrations come immediately to mind. One is alcoholic beverages. For everyone the question arises—is it right or wrong to drink? But the question must go one step further and ask—shall I by drinking put a stumblingblock in the path of anyone? Then he reflects that his example may be taken by many as endorsing the drinking habit. And so, at once, he finds himself thrown back upon the principle of self-denial or abstention for the sake of his beholders.

The same principle applies to all cases concerning conduct where others are affected for good or ill, or where the issue is in doubt. It can be applied to gambling, to smoking, to your manner of speech and conversation, to your use of Sunday, to your reading, to your amusements, to your mode of dress, and to many other situations.

> There is no place in the Christian life for the attitude expressed in the oft-repeated statement, "What I do is nobody's business." My neighbor is my concern. His welfare and salvation is my business. While we have a certain amount of Christian liberty, Paul warns, "Be careful, however, lest by any means this liberty of yours becomes a stumblingblock to them that are weak" (M. R. DeHaan in *Our Daily Bread*, December 21, 1961).

<u>LESSONS</u>:

1. We can never be free enough to be carefree.
2. If we are not on guard, our freedom may enslave us.
3. What is in our authority to do may become the stumblingblock over which another may fall.
4. As strong Christians, we are responsible for the example we set.
5. The restraints which Christ places on us are the restraints we, as Christians, should place on ourselves.

1 Cor. 8:10

The Danger of a Christian Making Himself at Home In an Idol Temple

> *Suppose, therefore, that someone were to see you, the one having knowledge* **of the situation**, *sitting to eat in an idol temple, will he not, being weak, have his conscience bolstered up to eat meat sacrificed to idols?*

How comfortable may strong believers make themselves at banquets of idolaters?

The apostle Paul produces an example of reality. *Eán* (1437), if, suppose, introduces the supposition of reality. In Corinth there were temples dedicated to idols where animal sacrifices were made and where frequent banquets were held. Among Christian believers, who were those who were most likely to participate in such banquets? They are described in verse 4 of this chapter, and were those Christians who believed that idols were nonentities in this world, in spite of the fact that they were considered as being real by the heathen. Paul later argues the situation further. In 1 Corinthians 10:20 he tells them that such sacrifices are to demons. They could not justify their conduct by the teaching that idols were nothing (v. 7). The question arises as to what happens to those people with tender consciences who do not yet have solid convictions concerning the unreality of idols?

Suppose, reasons Paul, an undecided person under conviction sees you sitting at a table (*katakeímenon*, the present middle/passive deponent participle of *katákeimai* [2621], reclining in order to eat) eating of the meat sacrificed to idols. He knows what you are doing. How will he be affected by your example? The verb *katákeimai* implies frequency and ease. It indicates that the person who reclines and is ready to eat is comfortable doing it. This practice involves not only eating the meat, but also making oneself at home with unbelievers who are idolaters. It reminds us of 2 Corinthians 6:14–16 where the apostle Paul says,

> Be not unequally yoked together with unbelievers: for what fellowship has righteousness with unrighteousness? and what communion has light with darkness? and what concord has Christ with Belial [a personification of unclean heathenism]? or what part has he who believes with an infidel? and what agreement has the temple of God with idols? For you are the temple of the living God; as God has said, "I will dwell in them, and walk in them; and I will be their God, and they shall be my people."

The question, then, does not apply only to eating or not eating the meats sacrificed to idols, but to what other believers will think as they see a fellow believer making himself comfortable with unbelieving idolaters.

Do Not Mix With Unbelievers

The apostle Paul is more concerned here about the effect and influence on seeing a fellow brother in Christ found in places where sacrifices to idols and their accompanying orgies of fornication, adultery, homosexuality, drunkenness, and other evils are common. Observe how idolaters are always mentioned along with fornicators, adulterers, effeminate, homosexuals, covetous, robbers, drunkards, revilers, extortioners (1 Cor. 5:9–11; 6:9, 10; 10:7, 8; Gal. 5:19–21; Col. 3:5, 6; 1 Pet. 4:3, 4; Rev. 21:8; 22:15). The verb that is used in 1 Corinthians 5:9, 11,

"I wrote unto you in an epistle not to company with fornicators" is *sunanamígnusthai*, the present middle infinitive form of *sunanamígmumi* (4874), derived from the word *sún* (4862), conjointly together, and *anamígnumi*, which is from *aná* (303), on, upon, again, and *mígnumi* (3396), to mix, and it means to mix together as being one. This is what the apostle Paul is warning us about, and not mere contact with unbelievers. In itself, the eating of meats sacrificed to idols is harmless, especially when one can fully justify such a practice in his conscience knowing that idols are nothing but imaginary gods (1 Cor. 8:4; 10:25–31). The more serious question is what will those with tender consciences think when they see confessing believers in places where evil abounds and is encouraged, such as an idol temple. As Paul says in verse 10, "The conscience of a weak brother is thus bolstered up." The verb which we translated "is bolstered up" is the Greek *oikodomēthḗsetai*, the third person singular future passive indicative of *oikodoméō* (3618), to build up. It is used also in 1 Corinthians 10:23: where Paul states, "All things are permissible for me, but all things are not expedient; all things are permissible for me, but all things do not edify [*oikodomeí*]."

It is to be noted also that *esthíein* is the present active infinitive of *esthíō* (2068), to eat. This suggests that the supposed presence of a brother in the banquet hall of idolatry may not be merely a one-time participation, but regular participation.

This supposition of the apostle Paul is what happens when a believer frequents places of immoral entertainment or practices that are foreign to the moral lifestyle of Christianity. The gospel is thus watered down, and those who follow us will believe that it is alright to frequent such places since we, as Christians, frequent them.

LESSONS:

1. As Christians, we should avoid places of immoral entertainment.
2. Even if one finds justification for his action in putting forth an excuse that idols are representations of nonentities, he should think of the influence it will have on weak believers.
3. Beware of excuses for entertainment or banqueting in places which in themselves may be harmless, but when weak Christians see us there, they may consider it as license to frequent them.
4. Although Paul, in 1 Corinthians 8:4, says that "we perceive that absolutely no idol in the world represents a real existence," yet in 1 Corinthians 10:20 he says that the Gentiles' sacrifice to demons, not to God.
5. In our Christian lives we should never do anything that would encourage those that are weak to engage in sinful practices.

1 Cor. 8:11 | *The Responsibility of Those Who Are Knowingly Stubborn*

*And the weak brother, **basing** himself on your knowledge, would suffer loss, although Christ died for him.*

Verse 10 provided us with the supposition of a mature believer sitting in an idol temple and eating meat sacrificed to idols, having clear knowledge of what he is doing. His reason is that idols are nothing since they represent nonentities (v. 4). He is indifferent to others and without love in this matter (1 Cor. 13:2), so this believer continues to participate in the temple feasts. The result may be destructive to himself. He thinks that it will not harm him, that he has a strong conscience, whereas it is a weak and stubborn one. His only excuse for his behavior is that he knows what he is doing. However, all that he proves is that he is proud in not recognizing the sinful practices of the past and giving them up.

Not only does he prove his own moral weakness by continuing in the practices of his former life, but he is putting in real danger any weak brother who may follow his example and practice. Now the apostle Paul tells us that his conscience is not only defiled, but it suffers loss. This is the meaning that must be attributed to the verb *apóllutai*, the third person singular present passive indicative of *apóllumi* (622), to suffer loss. While this is the best attested manuscript, it must be noted that the TR and the MT have *apoleítai*, the third person singular second future middle indicative of *apóllumi*, meaning he shall perish or he shall suffer loss.

In What Way May the Weak Brother Suffer Loss?

In this passage the verb *apóllumi* must be interpreted not as being lost forever, but that the weak brother suffers loss at the time that he sees another knowledgeably stubborn brother participating in the festivity of an idol temple. Remember, that this is a supposition and does not necessarily declare that a true believer was participating in such festivities. On the other hand, the verb *apóllumi* itself, in this context, cannot mean to suffer the loss of his salvation or of eternal life, but rather to suffer the loss of avoiding evil and seeking a pure and holy life. That it is impossible for a genuine, true, Holy Spirit-induced life of faith to be lost is clearly taught in the Word of God with explicit statements. For instance, our Lord said in John 10:28: "And I give unto them eternal life, and they shall never perish [*apólōntai*, the third person plural aorist middle subjunctive of *apóllumi*], neither shall any man pluck them out of my hand."

The loss that these weak ones would suffer is the abortion of the abundant fruit-bearing of the seed of the gospel. These belonged to the third type of soil described by our Lord in the Parable of the Sower (Luke 8:7) where we find the seed growing along with the thorns which finally choke the good seed. It concerns the struggling brother who in our verse is called the "weak brother," and translates *ho asthenōn*, the present active participle of *asthenéō* (770), to be weak. It represents his present condition as an assumed brother and, therefore, there can be doubts as to his spiritual condition to begin with. His faith is being developed, and its growth depends also on the example of other confessing believers. If such believers keep intimate company with idolaters and participate in their feasts, it may impress upon the sickly or the weak would-be brother that there is no difference between real Christianity and idolatry. The same apostle in 1 Corinthians 10:14 says, "Wherefore, my dearly beloved, flee from idolatry." Feasting with idolaters in the temple provides a bad example to others. The question is whether our freedom in exercising our faith is hindering or helping the person who is interested in the gospel to be attracted to the Savior.

"For whom Christ died" does not necessarily confirm that the weak brother is a born-again brother, for Christ died for all as Paul wrote in 1 Timothy 2:6, "He gave himself a ransom for all, to be testified in due time." And in 1 John 2:2 we read: "And he is the propitiation for our sins: and not for ours only, but also for the sins of the whole world." Then in 1 Timothy 4:10, Paul says, "For therefore we both labor and suffer reproach, because we trust in the living God who is the Savior of all men, especially of those who believe."

The apostle Paul in our verse under discussion is warning the proud, stubborn, confessing Christian not to become a stumblingblock in the exercise of saving faith of a so-called weak brother who may or may not yet be a true brother.

LESSONS:

1. The question we should ask ourselves when we are saved and living in an environment surrounded by sin is what will eventually happen to us if we continue in the sinful practices of our past life. To intellectually excuse practices by saying that idols are not gods is dangerous to ourselves and to others. At the same time we should try to enlighten our weak brother with the knowledge that is ours by God's grace.
2. Would my fellow man be turned away from Christ or my weak brother have his faith overtaken by the things of the world?
3. We should never, through our conduct, become an offense to those who would believe.

1 Cor. 8:12 | *Being a Stumbling-Block to Others Is Sinning against Christ*

Thus then, sinning against your brothers and wounding their own conscience when it is weak, you sin against Christ.

Since we are not an island unto ourselves and since our lives affect others as well as ourselves, we must consider the judgment of society upon our actions. In the case of the apostle Paul, he was concerned about the community of believers. How will our actions affect the testimony of the local church and its work?

Consideration Imposed by Love

One guideline of Paul's insofar as his actions and habits were concerned was the loving consideration of the brother with the weakest conscience. The question he always asked was, How might my habit affect others, and especially the weakest among my Christian brothers? Would he be tempted at all and would it be to such an extent as to weaken his walk with God? There was a stricter rule than personal comfort and gain that guided the life of Paul, and that was the rule of love.

Consider the Weak Conscience of a Brother

Three times in this chapter Paul is referring to those with a sensitive conscience.

In verse 7 there are the inconsiderate "brethren" who eat the meats sacrificed to idols, and their consciences do not bother them at all. However, this may defile the tender consciences of their brethren.

In verse 10 Paul brings the hypothesis of the would-be Christian who has knowledge that the meats were sacrificed to idols and reasons that because idols are nonentities (v. 4), he may freely banquet and eat such meats without consideration of what will happen to himself and others who see him. The first one (v. 7) claims that he may eat because his conscience does not bother him, for after all, idols are nothing (v. 4). The second one (v. 10) disregards the public example that he gives as he banquets with idolaters and enjoys their company. The weak brother who sees such an example is emboldened to do likewise, and his conscience is being destroyed (v. 11). So the conscience of the weak brother can be defiled and deteriorate instead of growing robust.

Now for the third time in verse 12, Paul speaks of such conduct of the stubborn, knowledgeable individual as sinning against others. The verse begins with *hoútō* (3779), thus, in this way; *dé* (1161), "then" as used in this instance; *hamartánontes*, the nominative plural masculine present active participle of *hamartánō* (264), to sin. The stubborn brethren who disregard the weak faith of their fellow Christians are actually sinning against their brothers, and the present participle indicates that it is a constant transgression.

Refinement of the Concept of Sin

Paul's concept of sin was refined. To sin was not merely to do something contrary to the law of God, but to do something that would cause a brother to stumble or not to be edified. Before doing anything, we ought to ask ourselves how it will affect a child in age and in the faith.

To the apostle, this particular problem about meat seemed in itself an easy one. So far as he was concerned, if the food was wholesome, he could feel quite free to put it on his table or partake of it as a guest (1 Cor. 10:25–27). The Corinthian Christians, however, were dealing with idolaters. They naturally shrank with abhorrence from anything that had been, however remotely, a part of a relationship which they now detested. They could scarcely reconcile it with their view of propriety even to touch that which had been connected with a service so vile. Such Christians would be pained and hindered if they should see other disciples doing what appeared to them as wrong. Probably, therefore, Paul's decision was that these brethren have uninstructed consciences in this matter. He determined to do all he could to instruct them, but at the same time he was not going to encourage the instructed believers to act with impunity, offending the uninstructed or would-be believers.

Paul does not say that it is one's only duty to instruct the consciences of other believers so that they could eat without a sense of guilt. I can perceive no essential wrong in eating such meat, Paul could contend, "but if meat makes my brother to offend, I will eat no meat while the world stands" (v. 13).

The Christian who chooses to do whatever his knowledge of a particular matter permits him to do without due consideration of his brother is transgressing in a more serious manner. He is considered as wounding (*túptontes*, the nominative plural masculine present active participle of *túptō* [5180], to smite, hit) the conscience of the sensitive. He not only sins against them by wounding their conscience, but he thus sins against Christ. This means that through the lifestyle of freedom that he adopts, he hinders what Christ wants to complete in their lives. Of course, if the Lord is the One who initiated the work, and it is His work, man cannot frustrate it, but he can hinder its intended growth (Phil. 1:6). This reminds us of the words of

Christ in Matthew 18:6: "But whoever shall offend one of these little ones which believe in Me, it were better for him that a millstone were hanged about his neck, and that he were drowned in the depth of the sea." Stressing man's responsibility in Matthew 25:45, the Lord says, "Then shall he answer them, 'Verily I say unto you, inasmuch as you did it not to one of the least of these, you did it not to me.' "

The sensitive brother experiences pain as he sees the stubborn brother dishonor God according to his own understanding of God's requirements. David felt that way when he wrote in Psalm 119:136, "Rivers of waters [tears] run down my eyes, because they [others] kept not your law."

Is the conscience of your brothers more sacred to you than your personal liberty? It is better to abridge our Christian liberty than wound our weak brothers.

What Are We Supposed to Do in the Absence of Explicit Instructions?

But what happens when there are no explicit, detailed instructions about particular matters in the society in which we live? How do we act in certain situations in which we find ourselves? How do we behave toward certain customs that exist in the community in which we find ourselves?

As far as Corinth was concerned, the Corinthian believers were of two backgrounds, one was the Jewish background and the other the heathen background. As far as the Jewish believers were concerned, what Jewish customs should the new believer in Christ keep? And as far as the heathen were concerned, which of their practices that were not evil in themselves should be kept and which should be abandoned? What about the behavior of the believer in a society having precepts (*entálmata* [1778]) that come out of human traditions, should we keep them or abandon them? Are there any rules whereby we can guide our conduct? Insofar as the heathen practices in which we (speaking of the Corinthian believers) were so imbued prior to our Christian faith, should we give them all up or should we maintain that which is not evil in itself, but which can serve us, such as eating the cheaper meat that has been sacrificed to idols?

In our modern society we are definitely facing such problems in our Christian life. We may come out of a religious denomination that has certain beliefs and practices. Should we abandon them all because we have been born again, or should we examine them carefully to see if they are contrary to the commandments of God? We may be saved out of the background of the philosophy to eat, drink, and be merry. Should we cut out all of these or some of them or what should be our guidelines?

Three Guidelines of Conduct

I believe the apostle Paul in Romans 14:2–4, 13–23 and throughout the eighth chapter of 1 Corinthians gives a number of different methods of dealing with such questions.

Some may take into account only considerations of personal information and enjoyment. Do I like it and does it please me? If the meat is good, and I want it, why refuse it? Even if self was the believer's primary consideration, he owes it to himself to examine whether or not it is really beneficial to self and others. Consider drugs, for instance. One ought not take them simply because they are pleasing, but must determine if they are destructive or if they will build character. Each individual must bear his own personal responsibility.

LESSONS:

1. What is your concept of sin?
2. Sin is not only doing something contrary to an explicit commandment

of God, but something that may hinder a brother's growth in Christ. That is considered wounding the weak conscience of a brother.

3. Sinning against a brother is sinning against Christ.

1 Cor. 8:13 | *Conduct Must be Determined by Its Influence*

For this reason, indeed, if food trips up my brother, I shall never eat meat, that I may not trip up my brother.

This verse begins with a conjunction that only occurs twice in the whole New Testament, here and in 1 Corinthians 10:14. It is the conjunction *dióper* (1355) meaning therefore or wherefore. It is expressed by the first part of the word, *dió* (1352), for which, for this reason, which is made up of the preposition *diá* (1223), for, and the neuter relative pronoun *hó* from *hós* (3739), which. *Dió* means "for which." The *per* (4007), indeed, a particle that expresses emphasis, is added to the *dió* making the conjunction *dióper* meaning wherefore, truly, indeed, wherefore by all means, or especially.

Doing Without Certain Foods

This emphatic conclusion is given at the end of Paul's argument concerning the duty of the informed Christian to consider the weak conscience of the fellow Christian who observes him and his conduct. For this reason, indeed, if food trips up my brother, I shall not eat meat forever so that I may not offend him. This is a general conclusion that we can make our basic rule of life. Eating or not eating a particular food that offends a brother does not constitute a necessity, nor will it lead to death. We can do without if that will benefit our brother.

The second instance in which the conjunction *dióper* occurs is in 1 Corinthians 10:14. In this chapter the apostle Paul discusses whether we should or should not eat meats sacrificed to idols (1 Cor. 10:19, 20). First Corinthians 10:23–33 discusses the freedom of each Christian to act according to his own conscience. However, there is something else to consider in determining Christian conduct. It is the conscience of one's brother. First Corinthians 10:29 says, "Conscience, I say, not your own, but of the other *that is different*."

Consider Your Own Conscience and That of the Brother With a Different Conscience

There are two things a Christian must consider. One is his own conscience which may be informed about certain matters and which may allow him to do certain things. He may have full justification and full knowledge that the thing he is doing is correct in itself and there is no prohibition against it as it stands on its own.

But the apostle Paul says to also consider the other man's conscience. What is translated "other" is the word *hetérou*, the genitive of *héteros* (2087). This refers to another who is different and, therefore, has a different set of criteria for his actions. He may not be as knowledgeable in his convictions and his judgment, but in spite of his conscience being different, it ought to be respected.

First Corinthians 10:29 then concludes: "For why is my liberty judged of another [*állēs*, the genitive singular feminine adjective of *allos* {243}, another but not necessarily different, simply another] man's conscience?" Thus the Christian has two consciences to consider, his own and his brother's. And since his brother's conscience may be different than his, what is he to do? He is to consider his brother's conscience as sacred and not violate it by pursuing a course that will be offensive. Verse 30 explains it: "For if I by grace be a partaker, why am I evil spoken of for that for which I give thanks?" In other words, I know that my liberty to eat certain foods is because of the grace of God which has been extended unto me. I can give thanks to the Lord for these foods. Why, then, not eat them? There is yet another consideration that enters in here. Whereas I can receive these foods as a gift of God and thank the Lord for them, how will my partaking of such food influence my brother? And the concluding verse is 31, "Whether, therefore, you eat or drink, or whatever you do, do all to the glory of God." Paul then closes with a general but basic command, "Give no offense, neither to the Jews, nor to the Gentiles, nor to the church of God: even as I please all men in all things, not seeking my own profit, but the profit of many, that they may be saved" (vv. 32, 33).

In Acts 15:29 the Council of Jerusalem clearly spelled out what was offensive to the Jews and what was offensive to the Gentiles: "That you abstain from meats offered to idols [the Gentiles' practice], and from blood, and from things strangled [a Jewish prohibition], and from fornication, from which if you keep yourselves, you shall do well. Fare you well."

In conclusion, what can be stated with certainty is that Christian conduct ought to be such that it gives no offense either to the Jews or the Gentiles or to the church of God. Respect another's traditions which have nothing to do with salvation. These are the matters in which we can differ and at the same time be brothers in Christ. However, the predominant law of love should prevail to respect the traditions of our national and community upbringing if these do not conflict with Christian doctrine.

Recognize There Are Absolutes in the Christian Faith

In our Christian life there are absolute commands that must be obeyed. In the context of the life of a Christian in Corinth, there were two such absolutes. The first absolute was one concerning fornication of which the apostle Paul said, "Flee fornication" (1 Cor. 6:18). The second concerned idolatry of which the apostle said, "Therefore, my dearly beloved, flee from idolatry" (1 Cor. 10:14).

Things Each Christian Must Decide for Himself

On the other hand, there are choices that each believer must make for which there are no commands, but they must be made in view of the consequences which they have upon ourselves, upon unbelievers, upon believers, and upon the cause of Christ. The question to ask concerning these decisions that each Christian must face is what will be the result of such actions in our own lives and in the lives of others, and particularly in the life of one who is my brother in Christ. Such is the case that is presented to us in 1 Corinthians 8:13. The suppositional conjunction *ei* (1487), if, introduces a hypothetical case separate from all experience and indicating a mere subjective possibility. It is different from the suppositional conjunction *eán* (1437), if, which implies a condition which experience must determine and involves an objective possibility referring always to something future. The "if" here in verse 13, therefore, introduces a merely hypothetical case that is purely subjective. If I meet with a brother of mine who is offended by seeing me eat a certain food, what should I do in a case like that?

If Any Food Offends My Brother

The word that follows this hypothetical conjunction is *brō̃ma* (1033), food, and not *brō̃sis* (1035), the act of eating. The fact that *brōma*, food, does not have the definite article in front of it would indicate that it refers to a certain kind of food although it is not designated.

The next word in the text is *skandalízei*, the third person singular present active indicative of *skandalízō* (4624), to scandalize, offend, be a stumblingblock in the progress that would have otherwise been made. The fact that this verb is in the present indicative means that my brother has made up his mind, and every time he sees me partake of that particular food, he is offended and his weak faith is polluted (1 Cor. 8:7). The weak conscience of my brother is due either to his lack of knowledge (1 Cor. 8:1) or to his lack of faith (Rom. 14:1). The two divergent attitudes toward food are distinctly spoken about by Paul in Romans 14:2, "For one believes that he may eat all things [the one with adequate knowledge]: another, who is weak [in the faith and not fully informed], eats herbs." The one, however, who is designated as possessing knowledge eats anything that is not explicitly forbidden or harmful. The other who is designated as weak in the faith, being persuaded that it is wrong to eat certain foods, conscientiously abstains from eating them. There is a natural reaction of the one against the other, although they may be brothers in Christ. The apostle Paul cautions against rejection of the weak brother by the one who eats, and judging and criticizing the knowledgeable one by the weak brother. Thus in verse 3 he says, "Let not him who eats despise him that does not; and let not him who eats not judge him who does not eat: for God hath received him."

It is the first scenario that is faced by the apostle Paul in 1 Corinthians 8:13. He assumes that one is a knowledgeable brother and his conscience permits him to eat that which may be offensive to a brother of his, possibly in the same congregation. The informed brother must then make a choice. He knows if he pursues his own conviction, he will surely offend his brother. On the other hand, he can deprive himself of the pleasure of eating the foods that he is lawfully permitted to eat. The advice given by the apostle Paul concerns the informed brother. What should he do? Proceed to enjoy his liberty in Christ to eat all that is available as long as his conscience does not bother him and knowingly offend his brother, or to suffer privation imposed by his will in spite of the permission his conscience gives him? The advice of Paul in 1 Corinthians 8:13 is that he should respect the conscience of his brother. His determination is expressed in his unequivocal conclusion, "I will never eat meat that I may not scandalize my brother."

Note that the verb translated "to offend" is *skandalízei*, the same word used in the first phrase where it is translated to cause to stumble and fall. This indicates an attitude that is determined as if it were a fixed conviction. If it were an occasional reaction to eating a certain food, it would have been in the future subjunctive *skandalísē*. Here I am, an informed brother knowing for sure that eating certain foods would offend my brother, yet I proceed to do so. To adopt an "I don't care attitude" is definitely wrong. In reality, these foods are not necessary for survival, but only for pleasure.

A Special Responsibility Not to Offend the One to Whom You Are Related

Observe that our verse says "offend my brother." In verse 11 it is "the weak brother" meaning any weak brother. And in verse 12 it is "against the brethren" meaning any brethren, but in verse 13 he speaks of "my brother." He speaks of an intimate brother, a personal acquaintance whom I know will be offended if he sees me exercise this privilege of my conscience. In reality, this is an expression of personal indifference, if not antagonism, to the one with whom the believer is related in the very intimate bond of Christ. The personal pronoun is also used in Romans 14:21: "It is good neither to eat flesh, nor to drink wine, nor anything whereby **your** brother stumbles, or is offended, or is made weak." The Christian life bears a certain specific responsibility toward anyone who is intimately related in a spiritual bond and who is "your brother." In order that such a relationship may be refined, Paul says in Romans 14:15, "But if your brother be grieved [*lupeítai*, the third person singular present passive indicative of *lupéō* {3076}, to make sad or sorrowful] with your meat, now you do not walk charitably. Do not destroy him with your meat, for whom Christ died."

Paul's Personal Decision

The apostle Paul comes to a very personal conclusion when he says, "I shall never eat meat." He uses the first person singular instead of the first person plural as in verses 8 and 12. He applies what he stated in Romans 14:3, "Let not him that eats despise him that eats not." Through example and exhortation, we are to "receive the weak brother" and not engage in doubtful disputations (Rom. 14:1). In other words, the personal decision of the apostle Paul is that instead of breaking fellowship with the weak brother, he would give up that food which is offensive. The enjoyment of one's rightful freedom is never equal to a harmonious relationship with a brother and a conscience free before God.

We must realize that this is a personal decision that the apostle Paul made, and it is not one that constitutes a command which must be obeyed by others. Paul was not a legalist. He did not believe that what he himself chose to do, for instance to work and not to be paid for the work that he did for the Lord, not to marry, and not to eat the food that offended his brother, should be made a law for everyone else.

The determination of his personal decision is expressed with two negatives: *ou* (3756), the absolute "not," and *mḗ* (3361), the relative "not." What is the meaning when these two negatives *ou* and *mḗ* occur together? In the translations this is expressed by "I shall not," a determined negative. I believe, however, that the meaning of these two negatives, the one absolute and the other relative, when used together indicate a personal choice in view of an absolute standard. The absolute scriptural standard for the Christian is that he should never live selfishly. But to live sacrificially is a matter of interpretation of how much one should sacrifice in this life to be the example that God wants him to be to his fellow human beings. At what point does a Christian cease to be selfish? This is a matter of faith and knowledge. There is a great deal of latitude and interpretation as to what each child of God should keep for himself and what he should give for others.

Each believer is the one to judge how many of the comforts of life he wants to enjoy for himself and how many he will sacrifice to meet the necessities of others. In every Christian community, there are those who are knowledgeable and those who are weak. There are those who are affluent and those who are poor. One does not have to be rich to be generous as Paul explains in 2 Corinthians 8:1–7. The poor Macedonians showed a greater generosity than the rich Corinthians. In all of these instances, Paul implies that the individual Christian has to make a decision as to his own way of life. And when he has made his decision, he has no right to look down upon his brother, and his brother has no right to criticize the one who chooses to live otherwise. There is an absolute standard set by God on selfishness and that is demonstrated by the *ou*, the absolute "not." There are things that are forbidden in the life of a Christian, and it is our duty to know what they are.

Many things are determined by individual conscience. It is the personal decision that each one of us must make. These are matters of individual choice and are represented by the relative *mḗ*, not, in the life of each believer.

Examine the Consequences of Each Choice

In our personal choices we must always bear in mind that there are consequences of every choice. There are rewards and retributions. Nothing that we eat or not eat will commend us to God (1 Cor. 8:8). On the other hand, we should remember what the apostle Paul said in 2 Corinthians 5:10: "For we must all appear before the judgment seat of Christ; that each one [*hékastos* {1538}, each one individually] may receive the things done in his body [during his lifetime], according to that which he has done, whether it be good or bad." Temporal decisions have eternal rewards. These rewards do not affect our salvation, but they do affect the quality of our relationship with Christ. The personal choices of privation and altruism will not be ignored by Him for whom we have made them. The apostle Paul was fully persuaded about the eternal rewards of personal sacrifices when he asked us to imitate him by saying, "Even as I please all men in all things, not seeking my own profit, but the profit of many, that they may be saved. You be followers of me, even as I also am of Christ" (1 Cor. 10:33; 11:1). The life of Christ was characterized by sacrifice and unselfishness. So was the life of the apostle Paul, and it is for such a life of conformity to Christ that he argues (2 Cor. 11:22–33). The choice belongs to every Christian separately. You can make your choices, but you cannot choose the consequences of those choices. The choice the apostle Paul made for himself was that he would never eat meat if that would offend his brother.

There are two distinct words that are used in this verse. First, it is the noun *brō̃ma* which means food of any kind, and then the word *kréas* (2907) which means meat, nonliving flesh. Undoubtedly, what Paul had in mind was eating meat sacrificed to idols which was sold in the open market for anyone to purchase and consume. The commentary on this is given perfectly in 1 Corinthians 10:23—11:1:

> All things are permissible for me, but all things are not expedient: all things are permissible for me, but all things edify not. Let no man seek his own but the good of another *who is different than himself.* Whatever is sold in the market, that eat, asking no question for conscience sake: for the earth is the Lord's, and the fullness thereof. If any of them that do not believe bid you to a feast [in their home environment], and you are disposed to go; whatever is set before you, eat, asking no question for conscience sake. But if any man say to you, "This is offered in sacrifice to idols," eat not for his sake that showed it, and for conscience sake: for the earth is the Lord's and the fullness thereof. Conscience, I say, not your own but that of another whose is different than yours: for why is my liberty judged of another man's conscience? For if I by grace be a partaker, why am I evil spoken of for that for which I give thanks? Whether therefore you eat, or drink, or whatever you do, do all to the glory of God. Give no one offense, neither to the Jews, nor to the Gentiles, nor to the church of God: even as I please all men in all things, not seeking my own profit, but the profit of many, that they may be saved. You be followers of me, even as I also am of Christ.

Not a Single Offense Against My Brother

The sentence with which the apostle Paul closes the eighth chapter of 1 Corinthians is, "That I may not offend my brother." The sentence begins with the conjunction *hína* (2443), in order that. In this matter of eating, we should always ask ourselves if that which we eat may trip up or scandalize our brother. Do not take anything for granted. Analyze your every action as to how it would affect your brother.

The relative "not" (*mḗ*) is used. It is as if the apostle Paul recognizes the weakness of our human nature and uses the relative "not" and is encouraging that every effort be made not to personally offend a brother. However, the success of this is only relative. No matter how careful a person may be, there are always some who are going to be offended. The aorist of the verb *scandalísō*, to offend, refers to a single offense brought upon a brother. The apostle Paul's determination was that he would not offend his brother at any time, not even once. But he realized, of course, that he was human, and he was likely to offend although he did not willingly do so.

We should all endeavor to live as Paul did, but at the same time recognize that we are dealing with human nature, our own first, and then that of our brother. We must never forget that although grace eliminates the power of sin, it does not eliminate the presence of sin in us or outside of us. It was the apostle Paul who wrote in Romans 7:20: "Now if I do that which I do not want, it is no more I that do it, but sin that dwells in me."

Living in the Light

In connection with that, we should remember the words of Christ in John 8:12: "I am the light of the world: he that follows me shall not walk in darkness [*skotía* {4653}, the consequence of darkness, or the sin which we inherited from Adam, the corruptibility of the body and the possibility of individual sin facing believers], but shall have the light of life." Christ is explicitly declaring that He is, indeed, the light of the world, and that we who are indwelt by His Spirit are indeed the light of the world also (Matt. 5:14). "He who follows Me," Christ said in John 8:12, "shall not walk in darkness." The "shall not" (*ou mḗ*) is the same expression that we find in 1 Corinthians 8:13. The *ou* is the absolute "not" expressing the desire of God, and the *mḗ* is the relative "not" which is the actual possibility facing every believer. Christ says that as far as He is concerned, we have moved from the kingdom of darkness into the kingdom of light. We are new creatures in Christ Jesus, but still, during our earthly lives, we carry in us the consequences of sin. We follow Christ imperfectly because of that remnant nature of Adam's sin. Our walking in the light is only relative. That is why the word which is commonly translated "darkness" is not the word *skótos* (4655), but *skotía*, the consequence of darkness. We, having received Christ, are the light of the world and we shall indeed have the light of life, but we must never fail to realize that we are redeemed, fallen human beings and our absolute redemption lies in the future (Rom. 8:23; see exegesis of 1 John 1:5 in *The Epistles of John*.).

LESSONS:

1. There is a special responsibility toward the person with whom we are intimately connected.
2. If my brother with whom I am well acquainted is offended by that which I eat or drink, I should consider giving it up.
3. It is better to give up a favorite food or beverage than to give up a brother.
4. Our conscience should be so tender toward our brethren that we try not to offend them even once.
5. The salvation of a soul is worth any personal sacrifice (Rom. 9:3).

Bibliography

General Works

Champneys, W. Weldon. *Things New and Old: Sermons Preached at St. Paul's and St. Pancras.* London: F. Bowyer Kitto, 1869.

Hastings, James and Edward, eds. *The Speaker's Bible: First Corinthians,* Vol. 1. 1927. Reprint. Grand Rapids, MI: Baker Book House, 1962.

Maclaren, Alexander. *St. Paul's Epistles to the Corinthians.* New York: A. C. Armstrong and Son, 1910.

Magee, B. "The Gospel and the Age." In *The Contemporary Pulpit,* Vol. 3. London: Swan Sonnenschein and Co., 1890.

Miller, J. R. *Devotional Hours with the Bible.* London: Hodder and Stoughton, 1913.

Redpath, Alan. *The Royal Route to Heaven: Studies in First Corinthians.* Grand Rapids, MI: Fleming H, Revell, 1960.

Robertson, Frederick W. *Sermons Preached at Brighton.* New York: Harper and Brothers, Publishers, n.d.

Shedd, William G. T. *Sermons to the Spiritual Man.* 1884. Reprint. London: The Banner of Truth Trust, 1972.

Lexicons, Encyclopedias, and References for Greek Readers, from Classical and Koine Greek to Modern Greek

Byzantiou, S. D. *Lexikon tēs Hellēnikēs Glōssēs* (*Lexicon of the Hellenic Language*). Athens: Koromēla, A., 1852.

Dēmētrakou, D. *Lexikon tēs Hellēnikēs Glōssēs* (*Lexicon of the Hellenic Language*). Athens: Dēmētrakou, 1954.

Enkuklopaidikon Glōssologikon Lexikon (*Encyclopedic Glossological Lexicon*). Athens: Morfōtikē Hetaireia.

Enkuklopaidikon Lexikon Eleutheroudaki (*Eleutheroudaki, Encyclopedic Lexicon*). Athens: Eleutheroudakis, 1927.

Kalaraki, Michael and Nikolas Galanos. *Iōannou tou Chrusostomou Ta Hapanta* (*Complete Works of John Chrysostom*), 1899.

Liddell, Henry George, and Robert Scott. *Greek–English Lexicon,* as Translated and Enriched by Xenophōn P. Moschos and Michael Kōnstantinides. Athens: John Sideris.

Megalē Hellēnikē Enkuklopaideia (*Great Hellenic Encyclopedia*). Pursos (Pyrsos), Athens: Hēlios.

Neōteron Enkuklopaidikon Lexikon Hēliou (*New Encyclopedic Lexicon "Hēlios"*). Athens: Hēlios.

Papaoikonomou, George L. *Lexikon Anōmalōn Rhēmatōn* (*Lexicon of Irregular Verbs*). Athens: Kagiaphas.

Stamatakou, J. D., *Lexikon Archaias Hellēnikēs Glōssēs* (*Lexicon of the Ancient Hellenic Language*). Athens: Petrou Dēmētrakou, 1949.

Works by Spiros Zodhiates

Conscience. Chattanooga: AMG Publishers, 1989.

Editor, *The Complete Word Study Dictionary: New Testament.* Chattanooga: AMG Publishers, 1992.

Was Christ God? Chattanooga: AMG Publishers, 1994.

The Epistles of John. Chattanooga: AMG Publishers, 1994.

List of Abbreviations

acc. (accusative)
act. (active)
aor. (aorist [2 aor. for second aorist])
cf. (compare)
ch. (chapter)
comp. (composition)
dat. (dative)
etc. (and so forth)
ff. (following)
gen. (genitive)
i.e. (that is)
imperf. (imperfect)
indic. (indicative)
inf. (infinitive)
KJV (King James Version)
MT (Majority Text)
mid. (middle)
n. d. (no date available)
N. p. (no publisher available)
NASB (New American Standard Bible)
NIV (New International Version)
NKJV (New King James Version)
nom. (nominative)
p. (page), pp. (pages)
part. (participle, participial)
pass. (passive)
perf. (perfect)
pl. (plural)
pres. (present)
pron. (pronoun)
Sept. (Septuagint)
sing. (singular)
TR (Textus Receptus)
UBS (United Bible Society)
usu. (usually)
v. (verse), vv. (verses)
vol. (volume)

Scripture Index

Mark

Luke

John

Acts

Romans

1 Corinthians

2 Corinthians

Galatians

Ephesians

Philippians

Colossians